Freedom and School Choice in American Education

Education Policy

Series Editors

Lance Fusarelli, North Carolina State University
Frederick M. Hess, American Enterprise Institute
Martin West, Harvard University

This series addresses a variety of topics in the area of education policy. Volumes are solicited primarily from social scientists with expertise on education, in addition to policymakers or practitioners with hands-on experience in the field. Topics of particular focus include state and national policy, teacher recruitment, retention, and compensation, urban school reform, test-based accountability, choice-based reform, school finance, higher education costs and access, the quality instruction in higher education, leadership and administration in K-12 and higher education, teacher colleges, the role of the courts in education policymaking, and the relationship between education research and practice. The series serves as a venue for presenting stimulating new research findings, serious contributions to ongoing policy debates, and accessible volumes that illuminate important questions or synthesize existing research.

Series Editors

LANCE FUSARELLI is a Professor and Director of Graduate Programs in the Department of Leadership, Policy and Adult and Higher Education at North Carolina State University. He is co-author of *Better Policies, Better Schools* and co-editor of the *Handbook of Education Politics and Policy.*

FREDERICK M. HESS is Resident Scholar and Director of Education Policy Studies at the American Enterprise Institute. He is the author of *The Same Thing Over and Over: How School Reformers Get Stuck in Yesterday's Ideas.*

MARTIN WEST is an Assistant Professor of Education in the Graduate School of Education at Harvard University. He is an Executive Editor of *Education Next* and Deputy Director of Harvard's Program on Education Policy and Governance.

Ohio's Education Reform Challenges: Lessons from the Frontlines
    Chester E. Finn, Jr., Terry Ryan, and Michael B. Lafferty

Accountability in American Higher Education
    Edited by Kevin Carey and Mark Schneider

Freedom and School Choice in American Education
    Edited by Greg Forster and C. Bradley Thompson

Education Reform: Coalitions and Conflicts (forthcoming)
    Alex Medler

Freedom and School Choice in American Education

Edited by

Greg Forster

and

C. Bradley Thompson

First published in 2011 by
PALGRAVE MACMILLAN®
in the United States—a division of St. Martin's Press LLC,
175 Fifth Avenue, New York, NY 10010.

Where this book is distributed in the UK, Europe and the rest of the world,
this is by Palgrave Macmillan, a division of Macmillan Publishers Limited,
registered in England, company number 785998, of Houndmills,
Basingstoke, Hampshire RG21 6XS.

Palgrave Macmillan is the global academic imprint of the above companies
and has companies and representatives throughout the world.

Palgrave® and Macmillan® are registered trademarks in the United States,
the United Kingdom, Europe and other countries.

ISBN: 978–0–230–11228–5

Library of Congress Cataloging-in-Publication Data

Freedom and school choice in American education / edited by Greg
Forster and C. Bradley Thompson.
    p. cm.—(Education policy)
    ISBN-13: 978–0–230–11228–5
    ISBN-10: 0–230–11228–5
    1. School choice—United States. 2. Privatization in education—United
States. I. Forster, Greg, 1973– II. Thompson, C. Bradley. III. Title. IV. Series.

LB1027.9.F74 2011
379.1'110973—dc22   2010048481

A catalogue record of the book is available from the British Library.

Design by Newgen Imaging Systems (P) Ltd., Chennai, India.

First edition: June 2011

10 9 8 7 6 5 4 3 2 1

Printed in the United States of America.

Papers delivered at a conference held at Clemson University and
sponsored by

The Foundation for Educational Choice
The Clemson Center for the Study of Capitalism

Contents

Tables and Figures

Tables

Figures

Foreword

Paul E. Peterson

The public school system that Horace Mann began to construct in 1837 now serves nearly 90 percent of those between the ages of 5 and 17. Consuming just short of 5 percent of the country's gross domestic product, it is the largest service delivery system in the United States that is directly run by the government. Growth in per-pupil expenditures—in real dollars— more than tripled between 1960 and 2008, and the number of adults working in the system for every 100 enrolled students doubled. Despite these additional resources, there is little sign of any gain in student learning. High school graduation rates are lower in 2008 than they were in 1970, and the test-score performance of 17-year-olds has remained unchanged since that time. If we can celebrate the fact that schools are no longer legally segregated, we must also lament that no further school desegregation by race has occurred since 1972. Disabled children (such as my own autistic child) now have a federally protected right to attend public school, but their presence on the scene can hardly explain the escalating costs or excuse the lack of improved learning on the part of other students. Undoubtedly, the productivity of the American school system is sliding seriously; with many other nations surpassing America's educational performance, it is nothing less than a national disgrace.[1]

Structural demands for reform have taken three forms—greater school accountability; transformation of the teacher recruitment, retention and compensation policies; and school choice. School reformers typically debate which of these three options, if any, can reverse education's productivity collapse. But this volume tacitly accepts the claim that choice and competition are necessary to change American schools in order to explore the pluses and minuses of the many forms of school choice.

Parents have some choices within the school system operated by the 14,000 school districts in the United States. Parents can pick their favorite district, or even their favorite neighborhood school, as long as they can afford to move into the community it serves. Magnet schools and open enrollment programs expand public school choices for a few others. But the more meaningful forms of school choice—those that take place outside the framework of district-run schools—come in five principal forms: charter schools, school vouchers, tax credits, privately funded schooling, and home-schooling. The order in which I have listed them is from the most to the least assisted and regulated by government. At one extreme, charters must be approved by a government agency before they can be established and receive per-pupil reimbursements for their operations. At the other extreme, homeschooling is ordinarily free of either government financial support or regulation, even more so than private schools, which ordinarily must be registered with a government agency.

Oddly enough, it is only the two extreme categories—charters and homeschooling—which are growing at a steady pace. School vouchers and tax credits are serving little more than 150,000 of the 52,000,000 students in the country, and private schools, though utilized by around 11 percent of the population, have not captured a larger share of the market for several decades.[2] Meanwhile, charter schools, nonexistent in 1990, are serving around 2 percent of the school-age population, and homeschooling, hardly known two decades ago, has captured about 4 percent of the market. If trends persist, the two together could have a larger share of the market than private schools within a decade.[3]

All the authors applaud school choice but they do not necessarily agree on what form it should take place, and much of the debate focuses on the charter school conundrum. Jay P. Greene is willing to support any kind of school choice—charter schools included—that gives parents more control over their children's education. He argues that only such an open-minded, pragmatic approach will have the political strength to succeed in the complex American political environment. If those who advocate school choice wait for "one best choice system," before lending their support to the cause, they will end up with nothing. Arguing along similar lines, Matthew Ladner says that only by making equity a political issue can choice advocates build the coalitions needed for success. He expects that enough school choices will eventually be carved out of the current system that district-run schools will be disrupted. George Clowes provides a detailed taxonomy of the many school choice options currently in place. He gives a positive nod to charter schools, though he does not think they can be a source of systemic reform.

Against these more pluralistic perspectives, a case for stricter adherence to free market principles is made. Greg Forster thinks we can support narrower school choice programs (such as those for the disadvantaged) only when they advance us along an over-all path to universal choice. Andrew Coulson suggests that charter schools may prove to be "dead ends" or "Pyrrhic victories" for the school choice movement. They can be easily regulated by the gov-ernment; they cannot provide religious instruction; and they offer just enough choice and are just barely good enough to drive private schools out of existence without giving the necessary impetus for systemic reform. Along the same lines, Pauline Dixon and James Tooley argue that the minimum essentials for an effective school choice innovation are (1) freedom for "educational entrepreneurs to open places for learning" and (2) parents must "have a monetary interest in their schools." They show that many very poor parents in some of the poorest communities in the world have found a way of paying for their child's education. In the strongest statement of all, Sheldon Richman draws upon classic economic theory to make the case that any government involvement—even school vouchers and tax credit subsidies—will "forbid full blossoming of the entrepre-neurial environment that is indispensable for optimal education." Better than any partial solutions is a commitment to letting the cur-rent system implode so that the country, in final desperation, will finally return to free market principles. One wonders whether the charitable tax deduction, an important prop for education's private sector, survives Richman's strict prohibition on any government involvement at all. In a similar vein, Bradley Thompson questions a child's "right" to a "compulsory" education.

It is easy to sympathize with all sides of the conversation that takes place within this slender book, especially when each perspec-tive complements the others. We all benefit from Richman's clear iteration of market theory, as he makes so utterly clear the distance school choice has yet to travel before it even begins to approximate that ideal. Dixon and Tooley's report of the passion for education among the poor in Third World countries is powerful and moving. Coulson brings his own refreshingly original international perspective to bear on the U.S. choice debate. Meanwhile, Ladner and Clowes provide informative, empirical detail about specific choice interventions in states and localities across the country. Leading off, Jay Greene's sparkling defense of all forms of school choice, including charter schools, provides a powerful motivation for the volume as a whole. Even Forster, who indicates he is anxious to speak as a counterbalance to Greene, acknowledges the underlying appeal of Greene's pragmatism.

Like the hobo, Greene is willing to take a crumb, even though he dreams of the place where bees buzz in Sycamore trees near a soda water fountain. In the land of school choice, we are all hobos—at least for now. But a read through these essays just might give us the help needed to hop on board a train going in the right direction, even if it is burdened by the heavy freight it bears.

Notes

1. The numbers in this paragraph are taken from the figures in Paul E. Peterson, *Saving Schools: From Horace Mann to Virtual Learning*, Harvard University Press, 2010, pp. 268–82.
2. *ABCs of School Choice 2009–10 Edition*, Foundation for Educational Choice, 2009.
3. Peterson, *Saving Schools*, Chapter 10.

Acknowledgments

This book grew out of a 2008 conference at Clemson University cosponsored by the Foundation for Educational Choice and the Clemson Institute for the Study of Capitalism. The editors and contributors wish to thank these organizations for the support that made the conference and this book possible.

Chapter 1

The Big Rock Candy Mountain of Education

Jay P. Greene

Lyrics of Big Rock Candy Mountain

One evening as the sun went down and the jungle fire was burning
Down the track came a hobo hiking and he said boys I'm not turning
I'm headin for a land that's far away beside the crystal fountains
So come with me we'll go and see the Big Rock Candy Mountains

In the Big Rock Candy Mountains there's a land that's fair and bright
Where the handouts grow on bushes and you sleep out every night
Where the boxcars are all empty and the sun shines every day
On the birds and the bees and the cigarette trees
Where the lemonade springs where the bluebird sings
In the Big Rock Candy Mountains

In the Big Rock Candy Mountains all the cops have wooden legs
And the bulldogs all have rubber teeth and the hens lay soft boiled eggs
The farmer's trees are full of fruit and the barns are full of hay
Oh, I'm bound to go where there ain't no snow
Where the rain don't fall and the wind don't blow
In the Big Rock Candy Mountains

In the Big Rock Candy Mountains you never change your socks
And the little streams of alcohol come a-trickling down the rocks
The brakemen have to tip their hats and the railroad bulls are blind
There's a lake of stew and of whiskey too
You can paddle all around 'em in a big canoe
In the Big Rock Candy Mountains

In the Big Rock Candy Mountains the jails are made of tin
And you can walk right out again as soon as you are in
There ain't no short handled shovels, no axes, saws, or picks
I'm a goin to stay where you sleep all day
Where they hung the jerk that invented work
In the Big Rock Candy Mountains

I'll see you all this coming fall in the Big Rock Candy Mountains

Asking market-oriented education reformers to describe the ideal educational or school choice system is a bit like asking hobos to describe the ideal country. You are liable to get an answer that sounds something like the Big Rock Candy Mountain. There will be trees that grow cigarettes, streams of alcohol, lakes of stew and whiskey, and hens that lay soft-boiled eggs. Or perhaps, if it is an educational fantasy we are indulging in, there will be no government-operated schools, no compulsory education, and no taxes or regulation. And why not? If you ask people to dream, they might as well dream big.

But that's silly, you might respond. Cigarettes don't grow on trees, you can't canoe on lakes of whiskey and stew, and there are no hens that lay soft-boiled eggs. Similarly, the government does, in fact, operate schools, does compel children to be educated, and does collect taxes and impose regulations. When we ask people to describe the best or the ideal, which constraints can they imagine away and which must still bind them for their answer not to be silly? Even the Big Rock Candy Mountain seems to recognize some constraints. The singer dreams of sleeping in barns full of hay, not in a waterbed with a down comforter. He recognizes the likelihood of going to jail, when he might just wish that he never broke the law or was never caught. In describing the best educational or school choice system, would it be any more unconstrained to wish that government wouldn't seek to reassert control over choice systems with burdensome regulations? Once we have broken the bonds of our current reality by imagining "the best," it's not clear where one must stop.

Describing the best also runs the risk of inviting futile debate over the particular characteristics of an ideal system that will never come to pass. Don't wish for cigarette trees, you might argue, because cigarettes are bad for your health. But can't one reply that in the ideal country cigarettes aren't bad for you? Or maybe you'll say that the

Big Rock Candy Mountain got it wrong because the lakes should be filled with vichyssoise and a nice white wine. Arguments over how large vouchers should be or whether transportation would be provided under the ideal education system are similarly futile. These are opportunities for plenty of fighting without obvious progress in enlightenment.

So how can we avoid the pitfalls of unrealistic fantasies and pointless infighting inherent in this exercise? First, we should not treat our ideal visions as if they were real things that will actually happen. We should keep in mind that they are just fantasies. Doing so will excuse some of our silly wishes while preventing us from squabbling over the details as if they were about to be enacted. But even comparing and discussing one's dreams can be very informative. From Big Rock Candy Mountain we at least learn that hobos have a taste for booze, good weather, and little work. Similarly, our educational dreams reveal something about us.

Second, our vision of an educational paradise serves as a road sign, indicating whether we are moving in the right direction and marking our progress toward that destination. We understand that in all likelihood we'll never reach the educational ideal, just as the hobo never arrives at the Big Rock Candy Mountain. But we can mark progress toward our ideal by that part of our vision that becomes reality. Done properly, the exercise of discussing ideal arrangements is not really about those arrangements but about the path that leads to better arrangements.

School Choice Paradise

With these guidelines in mind, here is my description of school choice paradise. Remember that I don't think this will ever happen, and because of that I feel free to be vague on certain details, since fretting over those details is pointless. The purpose of describing this paradise is just to point us in the right direction and describe what progress looks like.

At the heart of my vision is the understanding that education is simply an extension of child rearing. Educating a child is just a subset of all of the activities that are involved in raising him or her to be a successful adult. Parents have the primary responsibility for raising their children; therefore parents should also have the primary responsibility for educating them.

How did parents come to have the primary responsibility for raising their children? In part, parents have this responsibility out of respect for their liberty and autonomy. Without parents there would be no children, so we cannot completely disregard their interests in this matter. When parents bring children into the world, they do so with plans and preferences for them, which deserve at least some deference.

Of course, parents do not "own" their children, so we cannot completely defer to their plans and preferences. Children have some plans and preferences for themselves and certainly will develop more goals and tastes as they become adults. Respect for the child's development or future liberty and autonomy should also be a factor. The difficulty is that children are not capable or autonomous to take all of the actions and make all of the decisions for themselves. Someone else has to do it for them. But who?

This question has occupied great thinkers for centuries. How do we handle the half-way status of children as possessions of neither others nor themselves—persons not able to exercise their own liberty and autonomy but whose liberty and autonomy must be respected? Rather than rehashing the debates of great philosophers, I will make an empirical observation. Human beings have experimented with different arrangements for raising children over our entire history. Through a process of trial and error we have gravitated toward an arrangement that is the dominant practice in almost all places on earth and in almost all cultures: children tend to be raised by their biological parents who enter into a long-term relationship with each other. Those parents hold the liberty and autonomy interests of their children in trust until the children are able to exercise those rights for themselves. That is, we act as if parents "own" their children, confident that this arrangement is most likely to develop children into adults capable of having their own liberty and autonomy.

Throughout history people have tried other arrangements, but those civilizations have tended not to flourish. The experiences from alternative models for raising children aren't exactly carefully controlled experiments, but they have large samples and long-run outcomes. Children raised by their mom and dad tend to succeed while children raised by collectives or a single parent tend not to produce as much success.

Our confidence in the superiority of these arrangements is so strong that it is extraordinary for children to be removed from the care of their parents. In the absence of demonstrated gross incompetence or malevolence, children continue to be raised by their parents. This strong deference to parental care stems from a belief, supported by millennia of human experience, that children are better off being raised by imperfect parents than being raised almost any other way. In the absence of evidence of abuse or extreme neglect, we believe that parents—even ill-equipped parents—are better positioned and motivated to help their children become successful, autonomous adults than are others, even others with greater skills and expertise.

We could be mistaken in our confidence in the superiority of parents in raising children. But to dismiss the superiority of parents is to dismiss the wisdom of thousands of years of human experience. Some may be eager to dispense with these antiquated prejudices, as they would see them, for a brave new world, but I am convinced that these long-standing and widespread traditions deserve considerable deference.

If we think that children are best raised by their parents, both out of respect for the liberty and autonomy of the parents and out of a conviction that it is in the best long-term liberty and autonomy interests of children, then the education of children should be controlled by parents. Remember that education is just one aspect of child rearing. Reading with children in school is not fundamentally different from reading with children at home before bedtime. Learning values, priorities, and self-discipline in school is not fundamentally different from learning those qualities outside of school. We should no sooner interfere with parental wishes regarding these activities in school than we would at home. Parents have primary responsibility for raising their children, so parents have primary responsibility for educating their children.

Amy Gutmann, among others, has used the observation that children are not "owned" by their parents to assert the need for a sizeable role for the state, at least in the education of children. Since the future liberty and autonomy interests of children may be distinct from the plans and preferences their parents have for them, she argues, in *Democratic Education*, that the state needs to play a significant role in ensuring parents do not infringe upon the interests of their children.[1]

But it is revealing that advocates of this view restrict this significant role of the state to education. If they really believed that the state needs to play an active role in ensuring that children's interests were being protected, then the government's involvement wouldn't end at 3:00 in the afternoon. They should want the government to make unannounced visits to children's homes to ensure cleanliness, adequately stocked pantries, and an enriching environment. The fact that most of us would consider such actions by the government to be unnecessary for children and unreasonable to parents if they occurred after 3:00 in the afternoon indicates how unnecessary and unreasonable they are in education as well. And the fact that Amy Gutmann and others are unwilling to be consistent in advocating an active government role 24 hours a day suggests that they are not so much concerned with safeguarding children's interests as with rationalizing the status quo in education.

Unlike Gutmann, I am willing to be consistent in deferring to parents in the raising and education of their children. In my ideal vision, we would treat the dominant parental role in education the same way we treat the dominant parental role in raising children generally. In the absence of demonstrated gross parental negligence or malevolence, parents should assume responsibility for educating and raising their children. The state should only intervene if there is evidence of serious neglect or abuse, with respect to education in particular and with respect to child rearing in general.

I would only make two exceptions to this identical treatment of education and child rearing. First, the state should mandate by law that parents provide for the education of their children. Since failing to educate one's children, by definition, constitutes abuse or neglect, compulsory education produces almost no infringement on the responsibilities that parents already have. Of course, one could wonder, why not also have compulsory feeding laws or compulsory clothing laws? In essence, we do, since any parent who failed to feed or clothe their children would be guilty of neglect or abuse. The only reason to have a separate, explicit requirement for children's education is that failure to educate may be less easily detected than failure to feed or clothe. An empty mind is less obvious to casual observers than an empty stomach or an empty wardrobe.

Second, we should provide families with the resources necessary to ensure that each child receives an adequate education. I understand that we may not similarly provide families with the resources to feed, clothe, or house their children, so why do this for education? The cost of an adequate education is significantly greater than the cost to feed, clothe, or house children (keep in mind that the marginal cost of housing each child is modest and parents are already motivated to house themselves). Many families would be unable to fulfill their parental responsibilities with respect to education were they not provided with additional resources to do so. And since an adequate education plays such an important role in ensuring that children succeed and exercise their liberty and autonomy as adults, denying education to large numbers of children for lack of parental resources is simply unacceptable.

The state's role in education should be limited to mandating that children be educated and to providing the minimum resources necessary so that parents can educate their children. Beyond that the state should play the same role in education that it has traditionally played in child rearing: intervening only when parents have manifestly failed in their responsibilities.

At the risk of describing the ideal system in too much detail, I would envision that the state would provide a voucher to each child sufficient to provide for his or her education. If some children were significantly more expensive to educate, perhaps because of a severe disability, the voucher would be worth more. Parents would then be responsible for finding a way to educate their children with those resources as well as any additional resources they themselves may want to supply. If parents wished to use those funds to educate their children themselves, they should be free to do so as long as they can document that they are, in fact, fulfilling their responsibility of providing for an education. If parents prefer to contract with others to educate their children, they should also be free to do that.

The location, manner, and content of the education should be of no interest to the state. Where children are educated, how they are educated, and what they learn are parental responsibilities, just as where children are fed, how they are fed, and what they are fed are parental responsibilities. Unless the location, manner, and content demonstrated abuse or neglect, these are parental responsibilities. We defer to parents on these matters out of respect for their liberty and because we believe that parents are best positioned and motivated to make these choices.

Not Letting the Best Be the Enemy of the Good

My educational paradise may seem more like the Big Rock Candy Mountain than other visions that more closely approximate current arrangements for education. I fully understand and accept that my educational paradise is very unlikely to ever become a reality. Despite its impracticality, articulating this educational vision has important benefits.

In describing my educational paradise I reveal a few things about my preferences. First, I place a high premium on promoting liberty and autonomy. Second, I believe that parents are better suited to make decisions that benefit their children than strangers—even well-intentioned and well-trained strangers. The exercise of having to describe an ideal school choice system makes these basic preferences more explicit and transparent.

In addition, describing the ideal system clearly indicates the direction in which I think we should be headed and marks progress toward the ideal. According to the vision I've described, every initiative that expands parental control over the education of their children is a positive step and every initiative that restricts that control is a negative step. We'll never have the ideal parental control, but we can attempt to get more of it. We should be pleased with every increase in parental control we can achieve.

So, allowing parents to transfer their children among public schools within a district results in more parental control than simply assigning children to schools based on neighborhood. Expanding the choices to include public schools in other districts is even better. Adding charter schools to the mix is better still. Including secular private schools expands parental control even more. It would further enhance parental control if there were religious private options. Allowing parents to supplement vouchers with their own funds would expand parental control even more.

I am not describing the empirical effectiveness of each initiative, which can only be known from carefully designed research;

instead, I am simply describing their theoretical advantages. The fewer restrictions parents face as to the location, manner, and content of the education of their children, the closer we are to my ideal vision.

What if there were vouchers for private schools, but those schools were required to administer state tests? Advocates of testing requirements argue that testing provides necessary information to assist consumers in making intelligent decisions and ensures accountability in the use of public funds. But requiring testing as consumer protection is likely to be superfluous since consumers regularly demand that type of information even in the absence of a government mandate. And education providers in a competitive market are likely to be eager to provide testing and other information demanded by parents because that is part of how they can market their services. In addition, a government testing requirement distorts consumer information by insisting on a single measure when parents may prefer different or multiple indicators of school quality. Lastly, the only accountability that the public should demand is that students are, in fact, receiving an education. The location, manner, and content of that education should be left to the best judgment of parents, not the collective judgment of a test mandate. (Accountability testing within public schools is different because it is a management tool for the public system controlling itself, just as the Catholic schools may require testing of all of their students as a form of internal control.)

While it would be better if there were no requirement to test, even a voucher program with a testing mandate would expand parental control and should be viewed positively. Students would have more location options, and the restrictions that a state test imposes on manner and content would be no greater than the restrictions students already face in public schools. And if private schools found the testing unreasonably burdensome, they would be free not to participate. Vouchers with a testing requirement would represent progress even if it didn't represent perfection.

The point is that we'll never achieve perfection, so we should embrace every bit of progress that can be achieved. We have to be careful not to let the best be the enemy of the good. This is especially true since the best will probably never be achieved.

The opposition of some market-oriented reformers to proposals that would expand parental control, even with restrictions, is puzzling to me. As long as the expansion in parental choice is greater than the restrictions imposed, shouldn't we applaud the progress it represents? Their opposition is often presented as philosophical or based on principles. There are certain restrictions that these reformers simply cannot accept. But are the restrictions in the proposal worse than in the status quo ante? If not, opposing the proposal is just opposing progress.

Sometimes I suspect that the opposition to reforms with restrictions is actually based on prudential considerations rather than the ostensible philosophical reasons provided. The prudential calculation could be that if we resist adoption of a restricted proposal now, we might be able to get a less restricted one adopted in the future. And perhaps accepting limits now would set precedents that make it more difficult to produce more significant progress in the future.

Whether these prudential considerations are compelling cannot be judged in the abstract. The likelihood that holding out for more promising reforms will be successful depends on the particular context and political considerations. That being said, it has generally been the case that passage of choice reforms, even with severe limitations, has generally been followed by passage of more expansive choice reforms. Rarely has progress stagnated or been reversed (other than through the courts).

In Arizona, passage of one private choice program was followed by three more. The initial program in Florida was followed by two more. Iowa added a second program. Ohio added two more to its initial program. And Utah added a second program. In Milwaukee the private choice program started very small (capped at 1,500 students) and was restricted to secular schools. The program is now approaching 20,000 students and includes religious schools. Taking what you can get now has generally led to even more later.

Market-oriented reformers also sometimes have disputes over whether choice programs should be in the form of vouchers, tax-credit-supported scholarships, or tax credits for choice participants. Again, these are not really philosophical debates as much as debates about political strategy. Tax credits may be more likely to survive court challenges, but function almost the same as vouchers. Since the effect on parental control can be made to be identical whether in the form of a voucher or a tax credit, there should be no philosophical difference between the approaches.

The argument that tax credits are superior because vouchers are more likely to invite government regulation of private schools isn't very persuasive. The government does not need vouchers to regulate private schools. It can and does regulate private schools without vouchers. And there is no reason why government regulation has to accompany vouchers any more or any less than tax credits. If the reader remains convinced that tax credits have a political advantage over vouchers, I am perfectly willing to cede the point and alter my ideal fantasy. Arguing over these details is like arguing over whether the hobo's lake should be filled with whiskey or white wine.

Not Letting the Exception Make the Rule

Other market-oriented reformers might object that my vision of educational paradise has too few restrictions on parental control. What if parents were to seek Nazi or Jihad schools for their children? Shouldn't the state be able to exclude certain intolerant and oppressive options on the grounds that it contributes to greater tolerance and liberty in the future?

While I'm sympathetic with this concern, as a practical matter the attempt to devise government regulation of acceptable educational content is likely to be more oppressive than the oppressive education it might prevent. Very few parents voluntarily seek Nazi or Jihad schools. The dominance of Madrassas in certain countries, like Saudi Arabia or Pakistan, is largely related to the heavy subsidization of those schools by governments and the restrictions placed on other options.

The cultural preference for such an education also accounts for the presence of Madrassas, but this is something that government regulation is ill equipped to prevent. If the dominant cultural preference is for Madrassas, then we can hardly expect the government to develop regulations that forbid Madrassas. Even if it did, messages of hate and intolerance could be conveyed to children at home, so restricting it in school would have only a partial effect. Of course, if instruction at school or at home were sufficiently hateful or destructive, like encouraging children to become suicide bombers, then it would constitute abuse and be grounds for the state to intervene.

It is also interesting to note that as an empirical matter, there does not appear to be a strong relationship between a Madrassa education and terrorist activity. In a study conducted by Peter Bergen of the educational backgrounds of 75 terrorists, he found that 40 had attended college and only 9 had attended Madrassas. He also observes that all of the pilots and secondary planners of the 9/11 attacks had attended Western universities.[2] We give schools too much credit when we attribute to them all of the thoughts and actions of their graduates. Children are more strongly influenced by the values of their families and communities, making regulations of school content at best marginally effective.

The reality is that in a free society very few parents want to teach their children to destroy that free society. What's more, the broader societal influence from which children cannot be entirely shielded is likely to undermine the effectiveness of whatever destructive instruction children receive. The numbers of parents preferring Jihad or Nazi schools are small enough and their instruction is likely to be ineffectual enough that their preferences can be tolerated without danger to future liberty. Efforts to restrict these few intolerant educational options are likely to harm liberty even more as advocates would want to restrict Catholic schools for intolerance of homosexuals or restrict Orthodox Jewish schools for separating girls and boys. It is better not to get on to this slippery slope by not allowing the exceptional circumstances to justify unnecessary rules.

A Word on Politics

At several points in my argument I have made a distinction between prudential or political considerations and philosophical goals. For example, I've said that whether people should support choice programs with testing requirements is really a political calculation, not a philosophical one. If they can succeed in passing a program without the testing requirement, then opposing that provision is prudential. If they think that the testing requirement will rig the choice program for failure, hindering future expansion of choice, then they should oppose it. But if people think that a voucher program with a testing requirement is the best they can get and that it creates a condition for additional programs in the future, then they should accept testing requirements.

The only philosophical issue is trying to get more choice. The rest is a matter of political calculations and tactics. Of course, those political calculations and tactics are important, but they simply cannot be decided in the abstract. The principle that more choice is desirable can be decided without referencing the specific context, so I feel comfortable saying that more choice is better than less. But I cannot offer universal advice on whether testing requirements are always good or bad.

Nor can I advise whether tax credits or vouchers are best. Andrew Coulson plausibly argues in this volume that tax-credit choice programs have tended to be subject to less regulation, but there is no necessary logic behind that observed fact. It could easily change in the future. Again, nothing prevents the government from regulating private schools. The government can impose regulations with or without choice programs and whether choice programs are organized around vouchers or tax credits. The best tactics for avoiding regulations that hinder choice depend upon the particular circumstances.

So when people have disputes about whether to accept testing or some other requirements in a choice program, or about whether to structure programs as tax credits or vouchers, they are not really disagreeing about the goal of expanding choice. They agree on the principle, which really is the important thing. They just disagree over the best means for achieving that end.

While I offer no specific advice on tactics, which may disappoint some readers, I am very specific about the goal and how we should be open to compromise and gradual progress toward that goal. On some level this is a general statement about tactics—it is generally better to accept what you can get than to hold out for all that you want. I feel comfortable offering this piece of tactical advice because I think it is close enough to being true in almost all circumstances.

Not everyone agrees with this gradualist approach. Some folks insist that it is unwise or even unprincipled to accept compromises short of unhindered parental choice in education. I oppose that view for a few reasons. First, since the ideal will never be realized, holding out for it is (intentionally or unintentionally) a recipe for inaction and perpetuation of the status quo. Second, most progress toward the ideal of parental choice in education (or toward any other worthwhile goal, for that matter) has tended to occur by gradual progress. Revolutionary change almost never occurs. So waiting for revolutionary change is like waiting for Godot—it may never come. Third, revolutionary change is destructive and often has negative side effects. The keeping of tradition helps tether people to the common sense and wisdom of accumulated human experience. When people break completely free of those bonds they are as liable to do horrific things as wonderful ones. Sure, we have the American Revolution, but don't forget the French and Russian revolutions. Gradualism tends to be good.

A Word on Education

I've argued that the state should require that all children be educated but should be indifferent as to the location, manner, and content of that education. But people might reasonably wonder, what is the definition of "education" so that we can be sure that parents are fulfilling their responsibilities? A related question would be, What is the purpose of education, and how can we be sure that is being served by these arrangements?

I have to confess that I am intentionally agnostic about the definition or purpose of education, and I think the government should be similarly lax on these questions. Basically, anything that can credibly be claimed to be education should be accepted as such by the government. Any more restrictive definition would infringe upon parental autonomy over the location, manner, and content of education. Similarly, the state should and does have relatively lax definitions over what constitutes acceptable child-rearing practices. If the state developed an overly restrictive definition of "parenting," that would also infringe on parental autonomy.

I think we should be even more agnostic as to the purpose of education. If education is part of child rearing and if child rearing is preparation for one's adult life, then inquiring about the purpose of education is like asking what the purpose of life is. It's an interesting question, but one that should be pursued by people individually and not by the government. People will differ about the purpose of education, just as they will differ as to the purpose of life. It's not the proper place of the government to settle these disputes and impose any particular purpose on everybody.

Some might suggest that the state has its own purpose in education—to ensure that children will regularly obey its laws when they grow up. Of course, the government does have an interest in having its laws obeyed, but it is not clear that the educational system is a necessary or desirable part of ensuring that obedience. The primary vehicle by which the state ensures compliance with its laws is by deriving those laws from the people with their consent and by not infringing upon the people's liberty. Compelling students to learn obedience to the state in a particular manner is not necessary because consent largely ensures compliance. And it may be counterproductive because it may infringe upon people's liberty by regulating what is taught and how. The government's interests in education are best served by saying as little as is possible about what defines education and what its purposes are, and staying out of questions regarding location, manner, and content.

Conclusion

My vision of the ideal educational system is almost certainly as grand and unrealistic as the Big Rock Candy Mountain. I am only two steps away from saying that there should be no public role in the education of children. But while my goals are expansive, my requirements for a desirable educational reform are minimal. I only demand that a reform moves us closer to the goal of parental control, even if it is only a tiny bit closer.

It makes no sense to have an unrealistic ideal (as I do) and then reject everything that falls short of the ideal. That's not a reform agenda; that's a recipe for no reform at all. People who reject compromises that bring them toward their goals may take comfort in preserving their ideological purity but can never achieve progress, let alone achieve their ideal vision. I'll take what I can get.

While I favor compromise in practice, I don't understand why people would compromise in their ideal vision. If you are asked to envision what you most want, why bargain with yourself about your own dreams? Compromising the ideal vision gains no practical advantage other than sounding less silly than the singer of the Big Rock Candy Mountain. And compromising your dream runs the risk that you will distort your true goals and make unnecessary or unwise compromises in practice.

Be grand in your dreams and modest in your practice. This is the lesson of the hobo in the Big Rock Candy Mountain. He wants trees full of fruit, lakes of stew, and hens that lay soft-boiled eggs, but he'll accept a crust of bread if that is what is offered. We should do the same in education.

Notes

1. Amy Gutmann, *Democratic Education*, Princeton, NJ: Princeton University Press, 1987.
2. Peter Bergen and Swati Pandey, "The Madrassa Myth," *New York Times*, June 14, 2005.

Chapter 2

On the Way to School: Why and How to Make a Market in Education

Andrew J. Coulson

What Do You Expect?

The purpose of this volume is to identify the optimal way of returning parental choice and market forces to the field of education. But before we can properly design any system we have to know what it intends to accomplish. So, what do people want out of their schools?

On the basis of a review of survey and focus group research,[1] the public's aspirations can be distilled as follows:

- All children should have access to good schools.
- Schools should prepare children for success in private life, through a solid grounding in knowledge, skills, and values (specific expectations in these areas vary from family to family, though there is considerable overlap).
- Schools should explain the rights and duties of citizenship, to prepare children for participation in public life.
- Schools should foster harmonious relations among the different ethnic, religious, and ideological groups within our society, or at the very least not breed tensions between them.

It is worth noting that the above list captures the noblest goals of the nineteenth-century "common school" reformers—authors of the present U.S. public school system. Americans still want the things that education reformers were promising them eight generations ago. Can policymakers finally deliver on those promises today?

Where, and How, to Look for Answers

Public schooling has not fallen so far short of its promises, for so long, by accident. A large part of the problem is that the common school reformers who designed the present system approached education policymaking in a naive, unreliable, unsystematic way. That is not to say that they made no effort to study schooling in the United States and abroad. Horace Mann of Massachusetts, the first secretary of the first state board of education and leader of the movement, traveled all over Europe in the latter half of 1843, spending most of his time visiting schools.[2] But Mann had been appointed to the position six years earlier, and had long before settled on his education policy of choice: a system of schools operated by the state, free of charge, with state-appointed experts overseeing content, teacher training, and administration. In 1837, a month after his appointment to the newly created state board of education, Mann wrote in his personal journal that

> [i]t is the first great movement towards an organized system of common education, which shall at once be thorough and universal. Every civilized State is as imperfectly organized, without a minister or secretary of instruction, as it would be without ministers or secretaries of State, Finance, War, or the Navy.[3]

When he eventually set out on his European education tour, he simply fit what he saw into the policy framework he had already chosen. To avoid the copious disappointments that his preferred policy has wrought, modern education reformers would do well to study and understand the relative merits of alternative school systems *before* actually choosing which to implement. Fortunately, there is a great wealth of evidence on widely varying approaches to education going back to ancient times and spanning the globe.

Regrettably, interest in that evidence has generally been tepid among U.S. policy analysts and policymakers. The central objection to foreign education research is that cultural and economic factors differ so widely across nations that there is no way to tell if a particular country's educational success is due wholly or even chiefly to its system of schooling. That is certainly true. But there are ways of using the international (and historical) evidence that not only overcome this hurdle, but actually turn it into an asset.

The key is to identify so-called natural experiments in which either the type of school system is held constant while the cultural and economic setting varies, or the setting is constant and the school systems vary. In the first case, we can compare the outcomes of similar systems across many different countries and time periods. In the second, we can compare different systems of education operating simultaneously within individual countries, as well as observe what happened to educational outcomes when a given nation shifted from one approach to another.

If a particular approach to organizing and funding schools consistently works well across widely varying circumstances, and if it consistently outperforms other systems when operating in similar circumstances, we can be confident that this pattern of results is due to the system itself, and not simply an accident of circumstance. In fact, the greater the cultural and economic differences among the nations and historical periods studied, the more compelling any consistent pattern of results becomes.

Natural experimentation is used to great effect in fields as diverse as epidemiology and cosmology.[4] By applying it to the historical evidence and international research on education, we can discover reliable answers to questions that are otherwise difficult to explore empirically.

The Right Tool for the Job

Applying the method described above to a broad swath of human history, from classical Greece to modern America, led me to conclude in 1999 that free and competitive education markets have consistently done a better job of serving families and societies than have state-run school systems.[5] To test this conclusion, I subsequently applied the same approach to a new data set: the modern econometric research comparing school systems in developing countries.[6] An updated version of that literature review, expanded to include relevant studies in rich as well as poor countries, appears in the *Journal of School Choice.*[7]

Recent evidence, it turns out, echoes the message of the historical precedents. Figure 2.1 tabulates the results of modern studies comparing market and monopoly provision of schooling across seven different outcomes: academic achievement, efficiency (measured as achievement per dollar spent per pupil), parental satisfaction, the orderliness of classrooms, the condition in which facilities are maintained, the subsequent earnings of graduates, and the highest level of schooling attained.

As figure 2.1 makes clear, the weight of evidence is overwhelming. But what characteristics define the education markets that so consistently outperform state monopoly provision of education? Those defining features can be summarized as follows:

- Choice for parents
- Direct financial responsibility for parents

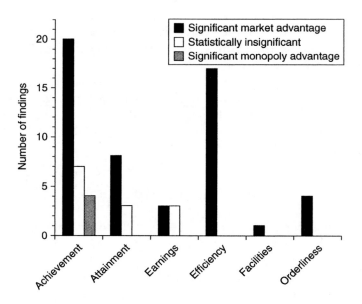

Figure 2.1   Market versus monopoly schooling. Number of significant and insignificant findings worldwide.

- Freedom for educators to set curricula, methods, prices, and admissions policies
- Competition among schools for the opportunity to serve students
- The profit motive for at least some education providers

A key premise shared by Mann and the other common school reformers was that state-appointed experts would make better educational decisions for children than would those children's parents. This premise has been repeatedly contradicted over time and around the world. From nineteenth-century England to modern sub-Saharan slums, even the poorest, least-schooled parents have frequently scrimped and saved to send their children to private schools when free or subsidized government schools were available. And the schools chosen and paid for by these parents have consistently outperformed nearby government schools despite spending considerably less per pupil.[8]

The benefits of parental choice go beyond improved academics. Unfettered choice has proven to be the best means of satisfying families' varied (and sometimes incompatible) needs and priorities, allowing parents to obtain the sort of education they value without imposing their preferences on their neighbors. The record of public schooling in this area is bleak. By establishing an official curriculum that is offered for free, state school systems create conflict among parents whose values and goals differ, pressuring them either to accept services that do not meet their needs or to wrest control of the system and impose their own preferences on their neighbors. Battles over sex education, instructional methods, school prayer, and the teaching of everything from the origin of the republic to the origin of species have been the inevitable balkanizing result.

Choice is of course meaningless unless parents have a variety of distinct options from which to choose. In order to create a vibrant and diverse marketplace, schools must have the freedom to choose their curricula, methods, and teachers as they deem best. The importance of this autonomy is well illustrated in the differing results one finds when comparing not market versus monopoly schooling but rather private versus government schooling, broadly construed. The findings charted in figure 2.1 compare minimally regulated private schools that are funded at least in part by parents with government-run schools that do not face serious competition from a private school choice program. Figure 2.2 broadens the scope of the question, comparing all forms of private schools (whether state funded or parent funded, heavily regulated or lightly regulated) with all forms of government schools (almost always monopolies, but sometimes systems facing real competition from large-scale private school choice programs). Taken together, these charts demonstrate that it is the freest, least-regulated private schools that enjoy the greatest margin of superiority over government school systems. The market versus monopoly comparison favors markets by a ratio of 15 to 1, whereas the private versus government comparison favors the private sector by only 8 to 1.

In addition to enjoying autonomy in their operations, private schools must be able to set their own prices. Prices governed by supply and demand are an essential part of free markets. They

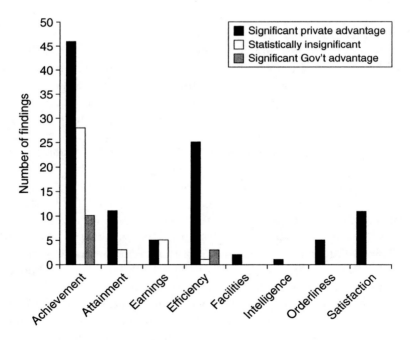

Figure 2.2   Private versus government schooling. Number of significant and insignificant findings worldwide.

simultaneously convey information about what consumers want and provide the incentive for producers to deliver it. High prices attract competitors who seek to profit by finding more efficient ways of delivering the sought-after service. This, in turn, drives the price down. Had it not been legal to sell the first CD players for $1,000 (roughly $2,000 in today's currency), it would never have been possible to justify or finance the research that turned them into $20 commodities.

Historically, the only school systems in which parental choice and school autonomy have long survived have been those in which parents directly shouldered some or all of the cost. Whoever has paid for schools has exerted pressure on them to conform to their desires and expectations—whether the payer has been an individual, a private sector organization, or a government. When individual parents pay for the services of a particular school, their demands only shape the behavior of that one school. Parents who want different things gravitate to different schools, preserving the diversity of educational options.

Under single-payer government systems, by contrast, the effect is to burden all schools with a single set of regulatory constraints. Governments set rules on what is taught and who can teach, on acceptable admissions policies and forms of business organization, and on the fees that subsidized schools may charge (if any). Interest groups lobby for the exclusion of educational content in government-funded schools that they find objectionable, and employee organizations lobby for policies that serve their members, narrowing the kinds of services that can be offered and impeding market forces.

Parents seeking educational options foreclosed by such regulations might in principle turn to unsubsidized private schools, which tend to enjoy greater autonomy. The problem is that in jurisdictions that offer significant government funding for approved types of private schooling, the unsubsidized sector tends to be squeezed out of existence. In many parts of the developing world, where the government's capacity to provide schooling is limited, the private sector still accounts for a large share of enrollment—sometimes an outright majority. In the United States, where private schools are mostly unsubsidized but government schools are lavished with $12,000 per pupil annually, the private sector has been squeezed down to 10 percent of total enrollment. But in the Netherlands, where a national voucher program has been in operation for over 90 years, unsubsidized private schooling has been reduced to less than 1 percent of total enrollment. The pattern is similar across wealthy countries that offer subsidies to private schools—the unsubsidized sector gradually shrivels up.[9]

Some single-payer education systems begin under a heavy regulatory pall. In Denmark and Sweden, for instance, the government imposed a core curriculum and rigidly controlled prices and admissions policies from the start. But even programs that initially had been relatively free have gradually succumbed to extensive and intrusive government control.

The Dutch voucher-like system was enshrined in the constitution of 1917, guaranteeing funding on a per-pupil basis to both government-run and participating private schools. The program offers equal funding to schools in either sector, though the per-pupil allocation is higher for special needs students and for those from migrant and/or ethnic groups associated with lower academic achievement. This program has suffered a relentless regulatory ratchet effect over time.

Before the 1980s, private schools had complete control over their school buildings during the hours the school was open for business. Government officials subsequently gained the power to allocate "underutilized" private school space to other educational purposes of their choosing.[10] During the 1970s, laws were passed stipulating how decision-making power must be allocated within private schools among management, teachers, and parents.[11] A national Common Core Curriculum was introduced in 1986 and updated with additional subjects in the 1990s.[12] Students' subject matter options have subsequently narrowed. In the 1990s, pupils could choose their exam subjects during the high school years, but by the end of 2002 the state had begun imposing set subject combinations and associated tests.[13]

The Dutch state's control over the content of voucher-funded schools has recently extended beyond curriculum to pedagogical methods, with teachers increasingly being assigned the role of "supervision and encouragement" rather than a more traditional role of instructing and guiding the educational process.[14] Over time, the state has also increased regulatory barriers to the entry of new schools and to the perpetuation of existing schools. "The current funding conditions are rather strict, and in recent years they have been changed to hinder the establishment of new schools,"[15] writes Benjamin Vermeulen of Vrije University. The minimum pupil counts required to create new schools (now 200 to 300 or more, depending on grade level and other factors) have been increased over time, as have the counts necessary for an existing school to remain in operation. In fact, current rules make it extremely difficult to establish new schools in areas already served by unpopular schools that have open places, protecting those incumbent schools from competition.[16]

The results of these policy shifts can be seen in the statistics for the creation of new schools: 74 were created in 1990, 67 in 1991, 13 in 1993, and only 5 in 1994.[17] Over roughly the same period, well over a thousand small schools were forced to either merge with other schools or close down entirely owing to rising minimum enrollment figures laid down by the government.

One Dutch teacher, who emigrated to Canada in search of greater educational freedom, told British Columbian researchers:

> The way it went in Holland when the government totally funds the schools...It seemed like all the time, well, the government started to dictate a little more of how the schools were run, and the people here quite remember that.[18]

It is critical to understand that this regulatory encroachment can be directly attributed to government funding. There is nothing in Dutch law that *requires* private schools to participate in their school choice program. It is perfectly legal to operate a privately funded private school in the Netherlands, and these schools need not conform to most of the regulations applying to government-funded institutions. The same can be said of other countries with similar programs, including Chile, Canada (British Columbia), and India. We thus have a natural experiment in which the dependent variable is the level of regulation, and the explanatory variable is the level of government funding. The clear pattern that emerges from this experiment is that governments from vastly different countries all regulate their private schools in proportion to the level of government funding they receive.

When parents pay for their children's education (referred to hereafter as "direct payment"), it has an important impact on school efficiency. There is evidence from developing countries that private schools funded by parents are more efficient than those funded by the state, producing higher academic achievement per dollar spent. In India, private schools fully funded by the state are consistently found to underperform those funded by parents. In Indonesia, school efficiency was discovered to be positively correlated with the share of local funding, derived primarily from fees paid by parents.[19]

A final advantage of direct parent funding over tax funding is that it eliminates a perennial source of social conflict: compelling taxpayers to fund forms of education that may violate their convictions. During the nineteenth century, when U.S. public schools were overtly religious in character, Catholics objected to paying for schools that taught using the Protestant version of the Bible. To this day, conservatives and liberals, pedagogical progressives and traditionalists, do regular battle over the content and methods of the government schools for which they are all obliged to pay.

While injecting parental choice into state-funded school systems reduces the pressure on parents to educate their children in a certain way, it does nothing to alleviate the compulsion of taxpayers. Under voucher programs, all taxpayers are compelled to pay for every legal type of schooling, regardless of their personal convictions. This proves to be every bit as socially divisive in practice. In the Netherlands, for example, many socially liberal Dutch citizens are uneasy with what they perceive to be the anti-Western, antimodern slant of the nation's conservative Islamic voucher schools. But, under the Dutch system, they are compelled to pay for these schools. The result is a zero-sum game: either voucher funding is revoked for conservative Islamic schools, in which case law-abiding Muslim families have their options curtailed, or it is not, and the deeply held convictions of the taxpayers are trampled.

It is easy to see how comparable divisions could arise within the United States under a voucher program. Would schools teaching that homosexuality is morally abhorrent and refusing to enroll gay students be eligible for vouchers? What about schools teaching that homosexuality is natural and morally neutral, and welcoming the enrollment of openly gay students? Each type of school could be expected to draw the ire of Red or Blue Americans reluctant to fund them, and precipitate efforts to regulate them out of the voucher program. Whichever side lost such a battle would be much embittered. When education is paid for directly by parents, this balkanizing situation is averted, because no one is compelled to pay for schooling they consider contrary to their values.

Amy Gutmann[20] and others have argued that official government school systems and the conflicts they generate are a necessary price that pluralistic democratic societies must pay if they are to maintain harmonious, civic-minded populations. Though this argument is presented as a piece of pure deductive reasoning, it is in fact an empirically testable hypothesis. More than that, it is a hypothesis that has been thoroughly tested and resoundingly disproven. When Patrick J. Wolf surveyed the extensive research in this field he found that freely chosen (usually, private) schools have superior civic outcomes than do assigned public schools. Of 36 statistically significant findings, 33 favored the private or otherwise freely chosen schools (such as charter schools).[21]

When students were asked to identify their least-liked political group and then asked whether they would let members of that group exercise such rights as free speech and pursuit of public office, only a single finding showed public school students to be more politically tolerant. By contrast, 11 significant findings favored students in private or otherwise chosen schools, and nine showed no significant difference between the two. The notion that social combat over a single official school system is somehow therapeutic for free societies is not simply unsubstantiated, it is clearly contradicted by a wealth of empirical evidence.

The combination of parental choice, autonomy for educators, and direct payment of tuition by parents ensures some level of competition, but the vigor of that competition depends on both the total size of the market and the number of different providers to which each family has access. The market for curricula, services, and reference materials aimed at home-schoolers, for instance, is vast, diverse, and innovative because the potential customer base is international in scope. From textbooks, to software, to satellite television broadcasting, to live Web-based tutoring services, the options are seemingly limitless. By contrast, the diversity in, say, the Milwaukee voucher program is limited to the 100 or so schools that can be supported by the local student population. And significant investment in research and development cannot be justified for a market that is capped in size at roughly 22,000 students (as is currently the case in Milwaukee).

Finally, the presence of for-profit education providers is essential for a genuine educational marketplace to arise. The importance of the profit motive is illustrated by the differing responses shown by nonprofit and for-profit education providers in response to accumulating demand. Critics of educational privatization frequently point to waiting lists at popular private schools as a sign that a marketplace would fail to serve many students and are of the view that schools, rather than parents, would do the choosing. Certainly, there is evidence of this phenomenon among the most prestigious private schools in the United States. Institutions such as the traditionalist Philips Exeter Academy and the progressive Laboratory School at the University of Chicago serve only about a thousand more students today than they did a century ago. This failure to significantly expand operations in the face of high demand can be explained by two factors: (1) the absence of an incentive (profits) sufficient to overcome the risks of expansion and (2) considerable funding from alumni intended to perpetuate a tradition rather than to commercialize a popular service.

There is, however, a for-profit sector in education, and it behaves in much the same way as any other for-profit industry. The most popular providers grow dramatically, opening new locations and often buying out less popular competitors. The after-school tutoring sector is perhaps the most familiar example of for-profit education. In 50 years, the industry-leading Kumon chain expanded from one student in one school in one country to 4 million students in 26,000 schools in 45 countries.[22]

It is worth noting that some networks of nonprofit schools, notably those run by religious organizations, have expanded without the lure of profits. Nevertheless, profits have proven to be the most effective and universally applicable force in disseminating popular educational services.

Ensuring Universal Access to the Education Marketplace

Markets are clearly the right tool for mass education, but in nations where people have both the means and the desire to ensure universal access to high-quality schooling, some form of third-party financial assistance is called for. In the absence of a state-run school system it is possible that this financial assistance would be provided entirely voluntarily through private philanthropy. In nineteenth-century England and the United States, before government entry into the education market displaced most private action, there was a vast philanthropic presence in education.[23] But those voluntary arrangements were less universal and often less responsive to families' demands than modern citizens would likely expect.[24] Could they be developed into something sufficiently systematic to satisfy the public's goals? That is certainly a worthy topic for scholarly debate, but for the foreseeable future there is no prospect that such a system would receive a serious hearing in the United States. After one-and-a-half centuries of state schooling, there is a presumption on the part of the American public that the state must ensure that sufficient funding is available for every family to see to the education of its children. Ignoring that reality is a recipe for policy irrelevance.

This leaves us with the most challenging question in the field of education policy: is there any sort of financial assistance program that can ensure universal access to a free education marketplace without destroying the conditions necessary for that market to survive and thrive?

The evidence already presented certainly identifies policies that are *not* likely to meet that test. Systems in which the state pays all educational costs for all families completely eradicate direct parental financial responsibility—a linchpin of the education market. But what of programs that provide financial assistance only when and to the extent it is necessary to ensure universal access to a quality education? It is possible to design both government voucher and tax-credit programs in this way; in the section that follows such programs are described and their merits explored.

Vouchers or Tax Credits?

The most obvious way for the state to ensure universal access to the private education sector is for it to provide parents with "vouchers"—checks that can be used to pay tuition at government-approved schools. An alternative approach is to offer K-12 education tax credits. The simplest sort of credit is one that parents can claim to offset their educational expenditures. For every dollar parents spend on their children's education, up to some preset limit, they pay one dollar less in state or local taxes. This amounts to a targeted tax cut on families who assume financial responsibility for their children's education.

Since lower-income families may owe little or nothing in taxes, the personal tax credit just described can be supplemented with credits for donations to nonprofit scholarship organizations. Businesses or individual taxpayers make donations to scholarship organizations, and those organizations use the money to offer need-based tuition assistance.

The remainder of this chapter examines the extent to which tax credits and vouchers meet the criteria for creating vigorous education markets and fulfilling the public's educational goals.

Preserving School Autonomy

Experience with K-12 education tax credits is limited to the United States, and goes back not quite a decade. Voucher and voucher-like programs have a much longer and broader heritage: over 90 years in the Netherlands, over 25 years in Chile, and close to 20 years in Sweden. What that history teaches, however, is that large-scale state-funded school choice programs invariably bring with them pervasive state control, either immediately or gradually over time.

U.S. voucher programs have lighter regulatory burdens than their foreign counterparts, but it is important to note that the U.S. programs are either recent or extremely small, or both. It is natural to expect that programs targeted at only a tiny segment of the population, particularly those regarded as "experimental," would be under less regulatory pressure than those operating on a grand scale and intended to be permanent. This is particularly true of the various voucher programs narrowly targeted at disabled students. Because of the profound learning differences among special needs students, and between those classified as disabled and those not so classified, and because programs targeted at this constituency are necessarily limited in size, pressure to regulate them is categorically lower than it is to regulate programs targeted at the general student population.

Since there is only one tax-credit programs currently targeted at this special population, it is necessary to exclude special needs programs them from consideration if we are to ascertain the relative suscepti- bility of vouchers and tax credits to regulation.

Even excluding such programs, all existing U.S. voucher pro- grams explicitly restrict student eligibility to a small subset of the population. Milwaukee's vouchers, for example, are limited to low- income children comprising less than a quarter of one city's student population.[25] The voucher-like "tuitioning" programs of Maine and Vermont serve only students in towns too small to have their own state-run schools, and both programs enrolled fewer than 7,000 stu- dents after well over a century in operation.[26]

These programs also impose important constraints on partici- pating schools that are not imposed on other private schools. In Milwaukee, participating schools must accept the voucher as full payment—a rigid price control. Participating schools forego any control over their own admissions policies, being obliged to accept voucher students via a random lottery. They may not require students to participate in devotional religious classes or activities, undermin- ing one of the chief raisons d'être of parochial schools. In Maine and Vermont, religious schools are no longer permitted to participate, though they had been eligible to do so before the 1980s. In Maine, private schools serving predominantly state-funded students must follow state curriculum guidelines. Vermont private schools are treated as "municipal employers" if they serve state-funded pupils, and hence must abide by collective bargaining and other provi- sions of the state's Municipal Labor Relations Act. In both of Ohio's voucher programs—one for low-income students in Cleveland and one for students in repeatedly "failing" schools in other districts— parental copayments are strictly limited. The Cleveland program also requires voucher applicants in grades K-3 to be admitted based on a random lottery if the school is oversubscribed, and regulates the length of the school day and year.[27]

Few of these regulations have been imposed on the nation's edu- cation tax-credit school choice programs (currently operating in Arizona, Florida, Georgia, Illinois, Indiana, Iowa, Pennsylvania, and Rhode Island).[28] Table 2.1 depicts the additional regulatory burden imposed on private schools participating in tax-credit and voucher programs (over and above regulations pertaining to all

Table 2.1 Additional regulation of private schools under U.S. voucher and tax-credit school choice programs, by category (excluding those serving only special needs students)

State	Program	Barriers to entry	Delivery	Staffing	Price	Religion	Curriculum	Test	Finances	Admissions
Arizona	Individual school donations									
Arizona	Corporate school donations							2		
Florida	Corporate school donations							3	2	
Georgia	School donations	2								
Illinois	Personal Use									
Indiana	School donations	2	3	1			2	2		
Iowa	School donations									
Iowa	Personal use					2			6	
Pennsylvania	Corporate school donations									
Rhode Island	School donations									
Cleveland, Ohio	Voucher	2		5	3			6		3
Colorado	Voucher	1						4	1	6
Washington DC	Voucher							4		
Florida	Voucher	2		2	6		2	4	1	6
Louisiana	Voucher	6				6		4	1	6
Maine	Voucher	2	2	5	6	6	4	4	1	6
Milwaukee, Wisconsin	Voucher	4			6	3	2	2	2	6
Ohio	Voucher				6			4		
Utah	Voucher		4					3	1	
Vermont	Voucher			2		6	4	4		6

Source: Andrew J. Coulson, "School Vouchers, Tax Credits, and Private School Regulation," Cato Institute Working Paper, October 5, 2010. http://www.cato.org/pub_display .php?pub_id=12198.

private schools in the given states). Empty cells indicate no regulations over and above those applying to all private schools, while progressively higher numbers (from 1 through 6) indicate progressively more onerous regulations in each of eight categories: barriers to entry, methods and timing of delivery (e.g., school year length, virtual versus physical schools), staffing, price, religion, curriculum, testing, and finances and admissions.[29]

Note that table 2.1 does not include a column on individual benefit (voucher or tax-credit) amount, because this affects only the number of families able to migrate to the private sector and not the freedom of operation of participating private schools. The impact of individual benefit amount is discussed further below.

As can be observed from table 2.1, tax credits appear to impose a noticeably lower regulatory burden on participating private schools than do vouchers. In a forthcoming paper employing multilevel regression to analyze this difference, I find it to be both statistically significant and large in magnitude. Furthermore, this finding is robust to an alternative ordinary least squares (OLS) specification that controls for possible confounding factors such as program age, dollar values of benefits, and dominant political party in the given state.

What accounts for this difference in the regulatory burdens imposed by vouchers and credits? The explanation that seems most consistent with the observed evidence is that legislators feel less pressure or obligation to regulate the way private individuals spend their own money than they do to regulate government spending of taxpayers' dollars. No one is compelled to claim an education tax credit, whereas all taxpayers must pay for voucher programs. (For a discussion of how personal use tax credits affect the general taxpayer, see the "Social Effects" section below.)

Preserving Parents' Financial Responsibility and Choice

To operate with the greatest efficiency and responsiveness toward consumers, schools must be paid for, as much as possible, directly by parents. Personal tax-credit programs clearly have the advantage over vouchers in this regard, simply because they let parents keep more of their own money to spend on their own children. This policy should thus be employed to its fullest potential. But personal credits are of limited value to low-income families who pay little or nothing in taxes. For these families some form of third-party financial assistance is necessary: either vouchers or scholarships funded by donation tax credits.

Even within this realm of third-party payment, there is reason to favor tax credits. As noted earlier in this chapter, single-payer education systems have historically ushered in a homogenizing regulatory burden. When there is only one payer there is one set of rules imposed on all schools, and families seeking financial assistance have nowhere to turn if their needs and preferences cannot easily be served under that set of rules. By contrast, scholarship donation tax credits create a multipayer system. While scholarship-granting organizations (SGOs) may impose conditions on the schools that parents can choose—just as a government voucher authority—the *multiplicity* of SGOs renders any such conditions less burdensome on parents. Conditions imposed on school eligibility by one SGO do not apply to scholarships offered by other SGOs. This allows parents to shop around for the SGO whose restrictions seem to them the least intrusive and problematic—an option that does not and cannot exist under a single-payer voucher program. What's more, the empirical evidence accumulated to date reveals the restrictions imposed by scholarship tax-credit programs to be few and far between—less confining than the government regulations imposed on voucher programs.

Social Effects

In one respect, both vouchers and tax credits offer a major improvement over state school systems: they increase the range of educational options open to families, reducing pressure on parents to consume educational services to which they might object. This allows parents to obtain the sort of education they value for their children without forcing them to impose their preferences on their neighbors, thereby eliminating one of the most persistent sources of social conflict in the history of schooling.

But there is another source of social conflict fomented by both state schooling and voucher programs that is largely avoided by tax credits: compelling all taxpayers to fund every type of state-approved schooling. As has already been pointed out in the case of the Netherlands, forcing taxpayers to fund schools that violate their convictions generates tensions among different ideological, religious, and ethnic groups. These are not only undesirable in and of themselves, they also provide an impetus for the imposition of regulations to eliminate contentious educational content.

Under properly designed tax-credit programs, taxpayers either spend their money on their children or choose an SGO to make donations. As long as SGOs are free to set standards for which schools they consider acceptable, taxpayers can opt to support only those that conform to their values. As noted in the preceding section, scholarship tax credits also serve to increase parental options when compared with single-payer education systems.

But what of the fact that personal use education tax credits, by virtue of lowering government revenue, place a relatively higher burden on other taxpayers (as compared with a scenario in which the government plays no role in education)? Does this mean that all taxpayers are being forced to subsidize the educational choices made by the families claiming personal use credits?

To answer that question, consider an analogous situation: under the federal tax code, charitable donations to churches are tax deductible. Religious donors thus pay less in taxes, other things being equal, than those who make no such donations. That means the general taxpayer must shoulder a larger portion of the cost of operating government than if charitable deductions did not exist. But neither the legal nor the common interpretation of these charitable deductions holds that they force general taxpayers to subsidize religion. Personal use tax credits no more compel general taxpayers to pay for someone else's education than charitable deductions compel general taxpayers to pay for someone else's religion. In both cases, general taxpayers are simply shouldering a larger portion of the operating costs of government, while those claiming credits or deductions are spending their *own* money on things of their choosing.

Financial Sufficiency

Another common criticism raised against tax-credit programs is that they would be incapable of providing sufficient financial assistance to ensure universal access to the education marketplace.[30] Certainly, it is possible to design tax-credit programs that suffer from this shortcoming, and indeed most of the existing programs fall into that category. But the same criticism can be leveled at existing voucher programs, which, while having higher average per pupil benefit amounts, serve fewer students.

What really matters, from a policy standpoint, is how many additional families a program helps to gain access to the education marketplace, and what its prospects are for growth in that area. This is a function of several factors, including the average benefit size, average private school tuition, the number of participating families, and the prospects for growth in that number. The program that will allow the most people to gain access to the education marketplace is not necessarily the one that has the biggest total dollar value (average benefit size multiplied by program enrollment), but the one that lowers the perceived cost of private schooling in a meaningful way for the most families. In that light, tax-credit programs fare relatively well vis-à-vis vouchers. Vouchers average a much larger benefit amount, but a much smaller enrollment and a slower rate of growth in enrollment over time. The highest enrollment voucher program, Milwaukee's, reached an enrollment of roughly 20,000 students in 17 years, while the tax-credit programs in Illinois and Iowa were enrolling hundreds of thousands in a fraction of that time (albeit with relatively tiny benefit sizes). The Florida voucher program is a leader in efficiency and growth rate, having reached 20,000 students in its first seven years and offering an average scholarship amount in the low thousands of dollars—sufficient to allow many families that would otherwise not have been able to afford it to send their children to private schools. Beginning in 2010, the cap on the total dollar value of credits that may be claimed is set to increase by 25 percent annually if donations in the previous year reached at least 90 percent of the cap in that year.

Moreover, evidence suggests that the ideal policy should ensure universal access to the education marketplace while maintaining a maximum of direct financial responsibility for families, so maximizing the average dollar value of third-party benefits is not inherently desirable. Third-party funding should be tailored to each family's needs, not universally set at a high, arbitrary value.

From a policy design standpoint, it is also easy to see how to create tax-credit programs capable of ensuring universal access to the marketplace. By combining personal use tax credits with credits for donations to SGOs, the pool of financial resources being tapped would be ample.[31] Model bills combining these two forms of tax credits have been proposed by the Mackinac Center for Public Policy in Michigan[32] and by Adam Schaeffer of the Cato Institute.[33]

This comprehensive tax-credit solution has in turn been criticized on the grounds that it ties funding to "the health of the economy and the generosity of the public."[34] As I have responded elsewhere,[35] the same can be said of all third-party payment systems operating in free societies, including vouchers and government school systems. While citizens must pay their taxes on pain of imprisonment, it is the citizenry that decides on the level of taxation it will bear. And in years of economic contraction, tax revenues are often reduced. Furthermore, it is difficult to imagine a scenario in which there was significant pent-up demand among parents for tax-credit-dona-tion-funded scholarships, year after year, with taxpayers remaining indifferent and continuing to spend their dollars on an unpopular government school system rather than on a scholarship organiza-tion of their choosing.

If voucher programs do have some theoretical advantage over tax credits in their ability to serve large numbers of students, as some voucher advocates claim, it has yet to manifest itself in the United States—the only nation to have tried both.

Taxing Concerns

Many supporters of school choice also advocate a flat tax structure with few if any credits or deductions, arguing that taxation should be used to raise revenue in a way that distorts taxpayer/consumer behavior as little as possible. This has led some school choice advo-cates to prefer vouchers over tax credits. Upon reflection, however, the desire to minimize behavior distortions induced by public pol-icy actually favors credits.

In the typical case, the introduction of a tax credit for some spe-cific purpose does skew taxpayer behavior, because the alterna-tive is to simply let taxpayers decide how much, if anything, they will spend for that purpose. But education is not a typical case. In education, unlike virtually all other fields, the government *already operates the dominant service provider* and not only tells taxpayers how much they must spend on education but pressures families into consuming its own services through its monopoly on the use of its education revenue (i.e., families pay zero tuition if they accept their assigned government schools, but must pay full tuition if they choose an independent school). Existing state schooling monopolies thus have a much more distorting effect on taxpayer behavior than any school choice program.

But while vouchers distort taxpayer behavior less than state school monopolies, they are still more problematic in this regard than are tax-credit programs. Under personal use tax credits, families simply keep more of their own money to spend on their own children, and as table 2.1 demonstrated, tax-credit programs impose less intrusive regulation on private schools than do voucher programs, causing fewer distortions in the choices families make. Under properly designed scholarship donation tax-credit programs—which allow SGOs to set conditions for the schools whose tuitions they will subsidize—taxpayers have real control over how their money is used. They can choose not to give money to SGOs that serve schools violating their convictions. Vouchers, by contrast, require all taxpayers to fund every type of schooling, which more severely distorts their behavior.

Even when SGOs are not permitted to set conditions on the schools that they can fund, they provide taxpayers with more latitude than do voucher programs. Under a voucher program, taxpayers have no escape from bureaucratic bloat or mismanagement. If the government program becomes corrupt or inefficient, they have no alternative but to keep funding it. Under a scholarship donation tax-credit program, taxpayers can shop around for the SGO they believe to be most efficiently run, and discontinue funding any that they worry may be corrupt. Therefore, anyone who wishes to minimize the extent to which education policy constrains and distorts taxpayer and parent behavior must prefer tax credits to both vouchers and state monopoly schooling.

Avoiding Pyrrhic Victories

A common belief among supporters of "school choice" is that any change in policy that moves in the direction of increased parental choice or competition between schools, however modestly, is desirable. In principle, there are two situations in which this belief would not hold true: dead ends and Pyrrhic victories. A dead-end reform would be one that makes it more difficult to continue advancing toward educational freedom in future, and a Pyrrhic victory would be a reform that brings gains in the short term but that ultimately results in a worse education system than the one that preceded it.

In the Pyrrhic category, consider charter schooling. It is well known that charter schools draw students away from not only conventional public schools, but also private schools. Moreover, some charters are created by the conversion of a private—even religious private—school to public charter status. In the short term, if the charter school law is initially fairly free, the net effect of this process may well be positive. Most families will have more educational options than they did before the inception of the program. But two things are likely to happen over time: more private schools will be forced by economic expediency to convert to charter status as the number of competing charter schools grows, and the charter law is very likely to accrete regulation as charters enroll a larger share of the total student population.

After all, the conventional U.S. public schools of the mid to late 1800s generally had more parental power and more autonomy than do typical charter schools today, but they have succumbed to ever-more extensive and more centralized regulation. If charter public schools follow the pattern set by conventional public schools, and if private schools continue to convert to charter status, what will be the end result? We could well see a heavily regulated state education monopoly that enjoys not a 90 percent market share, as it does now, but a 95 or even 99 percent market share. The end point would be worse than the situation we have today. While it is possible that charter schools will not accrete regulation like other public schools have as they begin to enroll a larger share of students, there is no reason to be hopeful in that regard.

The same Pyrrhic scenario applies to universal private school choice programs that impose curriculum and testing requirements on participating schools. The end result would be the assimilation of the existing independent school sector into the state-controlled sector, with little prospect for market dynamism.

The programs to avoid, then, would be those that impose market-killing regulations up front or those that have a very high probability of accumulating such regulations over time. The regulations that should cause market education advocates to walk away from the table should include mandatory government curricula or curriculum standards and the imposition of a single official test suite. Rigid price controls and teacher licensure requirements should also be viewed with great caution, as should the imposition of random lottery admissions.

A discussion of the harm done by price controls can be found in any elementary macroeconomics text, and it is widely recognized that public school teacher certification requirements merely constrain the teaching labor pool without improving student achievement.[36]

Though often viewed as being more benign, mandatory randomized school admissions policies also interfere with the operation of education markets. Specialization and the division of labor are core features of markets, responsible for the development of specialized expertise and the efficiency and innovation such expertise allows. Forcing schools to accept students at random cripples their ability to tailor their services to particular audiences, inhibiting specialization and the division of labor within the education sector. Moreover, not even conventional public schools are required to accept student by random lottery. In practice, public schools do *not* accept all comers. Public school districts frequently place difficult-to-serve students in specialized schools either within their own system or in the private sector. In fact, public school districts place hundreds of thousands of students in the private sector every year.[37] Even in the case of students without special needs, schools in a given district need not accept any student outside their catchment area. What the public school system guarantees is thus that every child will be served *somewhere*, not that every school will (or will be able to) serve every child. Given that random lottery assignment is not even required of schools operated by the state, it would be hard to justify imposing it on private schools even if it were benign, but as it is in fact deleterious to the operation of successful education markets it must be avoided whenever possible.

What about dead-end policies? There is a clear risk that the public and policymakers will be unable to distinguish between tiny, constrained school choice programs and genuine market reforms. When the weak choice programs fail to generate broad, dramatic improvements, truly effective market reforms could be mistakenly rejected along with them. Though the preceding sentences are written hypothetically, this process has already begun to unfold. Consider the disappointment with "markets in education" expressed by Sol Stern with regard to the crippled Milwaukee voucher program[38] or Chester Finn's criticism of "faith in market forces" with regard to *charter schools* in Ohio.[39] While it is too soon to call Milwaukee's program a dead end (it may continue its slow expansion and could eventually shed some of its market-killing regulations), that possibility cannot be dismissed.

The question for those who grasp the difference between genuine market locomotives and the toy-train policies with which they are often confused is what to do about it. Two alternatives present themselves: stop passing policies that cannot produce real market results or be much, much clearer on the differences between the two. Explain to the public and policymakers that if they want market results, they must create markets, and that if they persist in passing hobbled, minute programs, they should set their expectations accordingly. The second option should certainly be pursued with vigor, whether or not the first is adopted.

Conclusion

The public is fairly clear and consistent on its ultimate educational goals. The evidence is unequivocal on the kinds of education systems that most effectively fulfill them. The truly difficult questions are those of implementation, but even these are fairly tractable upon reflection. Whether or not it is desirable, there is no prospect that a complete abolition of state involvement in schooling will be politically viable in the United States in the foreseeable future. The task for policy analysts is thus to determine which school choice system can ensure universal access to the education marketplace while preserving the essential conditions for that market to thrive and survive.

A review of international and historical experiences indicates that large-scale state-funded elementary and secondary schooling invariably precipitates intrusive state control over that schooling. A review of U.S. experiences reveals that education tax-credit programs are consistently more lightly regulated than are voucher programs. Moreover, the odds that the current distribution of regulatory burdens would have arisen purely by accident are more than 16,000 to 1 against. Tax-credit programs not only draw a lighter regulatory burden, they maximize direct financial responsibility for parents—a crucial factor in the success of education markets. For these reasons, the combination of personal and scholarship donation tax credits represents the best practical school choice policy proposed to date.

Notes

1. See Chapter 1 of Andrew J. Coulson, *Market Education: The Unknown History* (New Brunswick, NJ: Transaction Books, 1999).
2. Mary Peabody Mann, "Life of Horace Mann," Washington, DC: National Education Association of the United States, 1937, Chapter 5.
3. Mann, p. 72.
4. It is also far from a new concept. The pioneering work with this method was John Snow's discovery of the source of London's cholera epidemics of the mid-nineteenth century: John Snow, *On the Mode of Communication of Cholera* (London: John Churchill, 1855). http://www.deltaomega.org/snowfin.pdf.
5. Coulson, 1999, Chapter 9.
6. Andrew J. Coulson, "How Markets Affect Quality," *Educational Freedom in Urban America: Brown v. Board after Half a Century* (Washington, DC: Cato Institute, 2004), pp. 265–364.
7. Andrew J. Coulson, "Comparing Public, Private, and Market Schools: The International Evidence," *Journal of School Choice*, Vol. 3, No. 1, 2009.
8. For the nineteenth-century English experience, see Edwin G. West, *Education and the State: A Study in Political Economy* (Indianapolis: Liberty Fund, 3rd ed. 1994). For the modern Third World evidence, see, for instance, James Tooley and Pauline Dixon, "'De Facto' Privatisation of Education and the Poor: Implications of a Study from Sub-Saharan Africa and India," *Compare*, Vol. 36, No. 4, pp. 443–462.
9. Chile has maintained an unsubsidized private education sector in which enrollment has fluctuated between 6 and 10 percent of all students over the 26-year history of the nation's voucher-like program, but Chile is a relatively poor country that cannot afford to offer vouchers worth anywhere near the tuition at these unsubsidized schools. Were it able to do so, Chilean unsubsidized schools would likely suffer the same fate as those in wealthier nations such as the Netherlands.
10. Estelle James, "Public Subsidies for Private and Public Education: The Dutch Case," in: Daniel C. Levy (ed.), *Private Education: Studies in Choice and Public Policy*. Oxford: Oxford University Press, 1986. p. 129.

11. Ibid., p. 123.
12. He-chuan Sun, "National Contexts and Effective School Improvement: An Exploratory Study in Eight European Countries," Ph.D. thesis, University of Groningen, 2003.
13. Verhage, "Reference levels in School Mathematics Education in Europe: The Netherlands."
14. Ibid. p. 4.
15. Benjamin P. Vermeulen, "Islamic Schools in the Netherlands," working paper, Vrije University, December 2003.
16. See further discussion of these points in Andrew J. Coulson, "Forging Consensus: Can the School Choice Community Come Together on an Explicit Goal and a Plan for Achieving It?" (Midland, MI: Mackinac Center for Public Policy, 2004).
17. Geoffrey Walford, "Funding for Private Schools in England and the Netherlands. Can the Piper Call the Tune?" Occasional Paper No. 8, National Center for the Study of Privatization in Education, Teachers College, Columbia University, November 2000.
18. Donald A. Erickson, "Choice and Private Schools: Dynamics of Supply and Demand," in: Daniel C. Levy (ed.), *Private Education: Studies in Choice and Public Policy*. Oxford: Oxford University Press, 1986. p. 105.
19. Coulson, "How Market Affect Quality," 2004.
20. Jack Crittenden, "Civic Education", *The Stanford Encyclopedia of Philosophy* (Fall 2010 Edition), Edward N. Zalta (ed.), forthcoming URL = http://plato.stanford.edu/archives/fall2010/entries/civic-education/.
21. Patrick J. Wolf, "Civics Exam: Schools of Choice Boost Civic Values," *Education Next*, Vol. 7 (2007), No. 3 (Summer), pp. 66–72. http://education next.org/files/ednext_20073_66.pdf.
22. Reuters News Service, "Kumon Ranks No. 1 in Tutoring by Entrepreneur Magazine's Annual 'Franchise 500,'" press release, January 14, 2008. http://www.reuters.com/article/pressRelease/idUS107596+14-Jan-2008 +BW20080114.
23. E.G. West, Education and the State.
24. A widely held view among religious charity schools in early-nineteenth-century England, for example, was that teaching reading to the poor would help to improve their morals, but teaching writing was unnecessary. There was some concern among the upper classes that if the lower classes could write they might use the skill to rail against the rigid classism of the times. Coulson, *Market Education*, p. 88.
25. Until 2006, enrollment in the Milwaukee program was legislatively limited to 15 percent of the public school district's enrollment. In that year, the cap was changed to a fixed value of 22,500 students. See School Choice Wisconsin, "MPCP Enrollment Cap," http://www.schoolchoicewi.org/issues/detail .cfm?id=10. Retrieved August 27, 2010.
26. Coulson, "Forging Consensus," pp. 22–23.

27. For details on the Cleveland program, see Coulson, "Forging Consensus," pp. 15–23. For details on Ohio's "failing schools" program, see Chapter 3301-11 "Educational Choice Scholarship Program," of the Ohio Administrative Code. http://codes.ohio.gov/oac/3301-11.

28. The regulations imposed under the Florida, Pennsylvania, Arizona, and Illinois education tax-credit programs are discussed in Coulson, "Forging Consensus," pp. 31–34. Iowa's education tax-credit legislation, passed in 2006, is described in "Senate File 2409" on the state legislature's website at: http://www.mvsto.org/pdfs/Senate%20File%202409.doc. Georgia's education tax credit, passed in 2008 as House Bill 1133, appears on the legislature's website at: http://www.legis.ga.gov/legis/2007_08 /pdf/hb1133.pdf. Rhode Island's program, passed in 2006, appears on the legislature's website at: http://www.rilin.state.ri.us/BillText/BillText06 /HouseText06/Article-024-SUB-A-as-amended.pdf. Minnesota has a tax deduction for private school tuition, but not a credit. It also has a credit for the cost of school supplies, but this cannot be used for tuition and hence does little to promote school choice. Therefore, Minnesota is not among the states that offers a K-12 school choice tax-credit program. If Minnesota were included, it would only bolster the point made in the text, since both its deduction and its credit impose few restrictions on private schools (being similar in their regulatory makeup to the Iowa personal use credit program discussed in the text).

29. For a detailed exposition of the regulation scale used here, please see Andrew J. Coulson, "School Vouchers, Tax Credits, and Private School Regulation," forthcoming.

30. George Clowes, "Still No Consensus on School Choice," April 1, 2004. http://www.heartland.org/Article.cfm?artId=16914.

31. As I argued in "Forging Consensus Comments by George Clowes and Jay Greene, with Responses from the Author," September 2005. http://www .mackinac.org/article.aspx?ID=7336.

32. Patrick L. Anderson, Richard D. McLellan, Joseph P. Overton, and Gary L. Wolfram, "The Universal Tuition Tax Credit: A Proposal to Advance Parental Choice in Education," white paper, 1997. http://www.mackinac.org /article.aspx?ID=362. See also Coulson, "Forging Consensus."

33. Adam B. Schaeffer, "The Public Education Tax Credit," Cato Institute Policy Analysis No. 605, 2007. http://www.cato.org/pub_display.php ?pub_id=8812.

34. Clowes, 2004.

35. Coulson, "Forging Consensus Comments by George Clowes and Jay Greene, with Responses from the Author."

36. Marie Gryphon, "Giving Kids the Chaff: How to Find and Keep the Teachers We Need," Cato Institute Policy Analysis No. 579, September 25, 2006. http://www.cato.org/pub_display.php?pub_id=6700.

37. Janet R. Beales and Thomas F. Bertonneau, "Do Private Schools Serve Difficult-to-Educate Students?," Mackinac Center for Public Policy, research report, October 1, 1997. See also "Jay P. Greene and Greg Forster, "Effects of Funding Incentives on Special Education Enrollment," Manhattan Institute Civic Report No. 32, December 2002.
38. Sol Stern, "School Choice Isn't Enough," *City Journal*, Vol. 18 (2008), No. 1. http://www.city-journal.org/2008/18_1_instructional_reform.html.
39. Chester Finn, "Charter schools need more than money," *Columbus Dispatch*, December 31, 2007. http://columbusdispatch.com/live/content /editorials/stories/2007/12/31/Frost-Brooks___ART_12-31-07_A8 _FI8T71D.html?sid=101.

Chapter 3

The Design of School Choice Programs: A Systems Approach

George A. Clowes

"Cheshire Puss," [Alice] began... "Would you tell me, please, which way I ought to walk from here?"
"That depends a good deal on where you want to get to," said the Cat.
"I don't much care where—" said Alice.
"Then it doesn't matter which way you walk," said the Cat.[1]

Aims and Objectives: Education and a Free Society

"What is the best way to design school choice programs?" To answer this question, we first need to define our objectives, for both school choice and public education: Where do we want to go? What do we want to accomplish? How are we currently attempting to achieve those objectives? In any policy development, it is essential not only to have a clear idea of the problem to be addressed, but also to have a clear idea of the objective of the system where the problem is occurring *and* the objective of the wider system.[2] In the present context, this requires first addressing the question of what is the goal of school choice, and what is the overall goal of public education.

Education is important in contributing to economic growth, it is needed to develop adults who can accept responsibility and earn a living, and it helps people lead healthier, more satisfying, and culturally richer lives. However, none of these is the reason why elementary and secondary education ought to be encouraged, subsidized, or of particular interest to governments in the United States. Many pursuits are good for individuals or society as a whole but do not fall within the limited set of powers given to the national government by the U.S. Constitution, nor would the founding fathers have thought them deserving of support by state or local governments (which are not similarly constrained by the Constitution). Elementary and secondary education rises to the level of an activity that merits government encouragement because the American system of governance requires an educated public.

Thomas Jefferson said: "If a nation expects to be ignorant and free, in a state of civilization, it expects what never was and never will be." Similarly, founder John Adams advised, "Children should be educated and instructed in the principles of freedom." State support for schools was one of the earliest types of expenditure common in the colonies. The first school in America, the Boston Latin School founded in 1635, was tax funded.[3] Tax-funded schools opened soon afterward in Charlestown and Dorchester. Today, all state constitutions provide for free education for all children.

Governments in free societies have a legitimate interest in ensuring the conditions needed to sustain their existence for "ourselves and our posterity." The ultimate goal being addressed by school reformers, then, is not merely higher test scores or "better schools," but the continued existence of our republican form of government. It is critically important to have a well-educated populace in the United States because that is a prerequisite for sustaining a free society into the future. The United States of America is based on a set of ideas that are laid out in the Declaration of Independence—the "catechism" of American citizenship, according to George Will—and the nation's continued existence depends on its citizens understanding those ideas as the fundamental basis for being an American.[4]

The question then is, How do we get a well-educated populace? Today we rely heavily on a system of taxpayer-financed, government-owned, government-run, and government-staffed schools, with oversight and monitoring by the government and with standards of performance set by the government. It is a system that was adopted haphazardly, mostly put in place at the end of the nineteenth century, the result of prejudices and private interest group pressures and the limited knowledge and technologies of the time. No one put in charge of designing a school system for a free society today would come up with a plan resembling the system currently in place.

In 1955, Milton Friedman proposed a different way of organizing the provision of this free K-12 education that would be more consistent with the principles of a free society.[5] Friedman examined the role of government in providing services and noted a failure to distinguish between activities that it was appropriate for the government to finance and activities that it was appropriate for the government to administer.

"Government has appropriately financed general education for citizenship, but in the process it has been led also to administer most of the schools that provide such education," wrote Friedman. "Yet...the administration of schools is neither required by the financing of education, nor justifiable in its own right in a predominantly free enterprise society."

Since parents are able to send their children to government schools without any special payment, very few can or will send them to other schools unless they receive a subsidy, noted Friedman. However, if the subsidy—in the form of a school voucher—were made available to parents regardless of which school their children attended, he predicted "a wide variety of schools" would spring up to meet the demand. Parents would then be able to directly convey their views about different schools by transferring their children from one school to another, provided the chosen schools met a set of minimum specified standards. A system of school vouchers would widen the range of choices available to parents, argued Friedman, since parents would no longer have to change their place of residence in order to change their child's subsidized school.

Friedman's objective in developing his voucher proposal was not in reaction to any perceived deficiencies in the quality of the public schools at that time but to enhance individual freedom. As Krista Kafer of the Independence Institute recently noted, while school choice benefits individual students and provides an incentive for systemic reform, these benefits "are secondary to the primary virtue of education choice—freedom."[6]

Development of the School Choice Concept

The essential features of Friedman's 1955 voucher proposal are as follows:

- Vouchers would be available to all children.
- The money would follow the child to the school chosen by their parents.
- Vouchers would be worth the cost of educating a child in the public schools.
- Add-on fees would be permitted.
- For-profit, not-for-profit, and religious schools would be allowed to participate.
- A minimum of standards would be imposed on participating schools.
- In the free market created by vouchers, competition would produce a variety of schools for parents to choose from.
- Vouchers would relieve the double-payment burden for parents who send their children to private schools.
- The fundamental objective of vouchers would be systemic reform—to reform the system for delivering K-12 education to one more consistent with the principles of a free society.

To date, this "universal" voucher concept has not been implemented anywhere. Indeed, Friedman's idea did not gain traction for over 30 years, until 1989. It was then that Wisconsin State Rep. Polly Williams from Milwaukee, a Democrat, pushed through a voucher program targeting children from low-income families in Milwaukee. A modern voucher program was now in existence—the Milwaukee Parental Choice Program—but the features of the voucher were not the same as those in Friedman's original vision:

- The Milwaukee voucher is limited to use by low-income families.
- The Milwaukee voucher has a value of only half the public school spending.
- Add-on fees are not allowed.
- Enrollment in the program is capped at an arbitrary low level.

- Only secular private schools were originally allowed to participate, although religious schools were subsequently added to the program.
- The primary objective of the Milwaukee voucher is to rescue individual children from the city's failing public schools and enable their parents to transfer them to an alternative private school.

Following the creation of the Milwaukee Parental Choice Program, additional voucher programs involving the participation of private schools were established in Cleveland, Ohio, in Florida, in New Orleans, Louisiana, and—until terminated by the 111th Congress in 2009—in Washington, DC. State legislatures in Florida, Colorado, and Utah approved other voucher programs but these were struck down by the courts or by voter referendum. However, two other programs that predated Friedman's proposal continued in operation; these were the "tuitioning" programs that some small school districts in Maine and Vermont had maintained since the nineteenth century. These programs provide school vouchers to students whose local communities (typically small towns) choose not to maintain their own public schools.

Following Friedman's voucher proposal, other voucher-like school choice programs have been developed where the per-pupil funding—or at least a major portion of it—follows the child to the school chosen by their parents but where the choice of schools is limited to other public schools. For example, open enrollment—where parents may choose schools across district lines—has been adopted in several states. Weighted Student Funding is a type of public school choice program that allows parents to choose from public schools within a school district. Charter schools offer yet another variety of public school choice, where funding follows the child to a public school that is operated by a private entity, not by the local school board.

Vouchers and the public school choice options described above all involve bringing parents into the process of allocating existing educational resources to individual schools. Instead of having a school district administrator make those decisions, vouchers and public school choice allow parents to make those decisions. With Weighted Student Funding, parents decide how funds will be allocated among district schools; with open enrollment and charter schools, parents decide how much funding will flow out of the district to other public schools; and with vouchers, parents decide how much funding will flow out of the district to private schools.

It is possible to design nonvoucher programs where parents direct the flow of some of their education tax dollars to private schools. For example, in a 1988 book from The Heartland Institute, *We Can Rescue Our Children*, a school choice program involving property tax rebates was proposed for Chicago.[7] The plan would have permitted parents to obtain a rebate check for their education-related property taxes to offset the cost of private school tuition. Low-income families were included in the plan through a renter rebate option, since renters also pay property taxes via their rent. Businesses and extended family members also could obtain a rebate of a portion of their education-related property taxes for donations they made to support private schools or individual student tuition. However, this rebate plan, which would have been relatively easy to administer, was never implemented.

Instead, another type of education tax relief program—tax credits—gained favor among school reformers. Tax credits, like rebates, address the double-payment issue that public school choice fails to address, but tend to be more complex to administer. They are generally of two kinds. The first is an individual tax credit where parents can reduce their tax liability based on the amount of educational expenses they have incurred in educating their child outside of the public schools, either at a private school or through homeschooling. The second is where taxpayers can reduce their tax liability based on the amount they contribute to organizations that provide private school tuition scholarships, usually for children in low-income families.

While tax credits enable parents to exercise school choice, they differ from vouchers and the Heartland tax rebates in one very important respect: they do not involve parents in the direct allocation of current education resources to alternative schools. Instead, they establish an alternative funding mechanism for private school tuition, one that is entirely separate from the mechanism for funding the public schools. Rather than seeking an allocation of per-pupil funds from the current pool of K-12 education dollars, tax credits require the state to forego the collection of tax dollars—usually from the General Fund—to leave parents with more of their own money to choose an alternative means of schooling their child.

Thus, tax credits have somewhat different objectives than universal or targeted vouchers, where education funding follows the child. The objectives of tax credits are threefold:

- First, to provide relief for the double payment for education that parents incur when they choose not to have their children educated in the public schools.
- Second, to establish an alternative source of funding for non-public K-12 educational expenses.
- Third, to provide a variety of means for making those funds available to low-income families as well as to those with substantial tax liabilities, that is, via refundable credits and scholarships.

During the development of this range of programs, school choice began to involve two overall aims. The first and rather obvious aim is to provide parents with an opportunity to transfer their child from one school to another; this aim is defined here as the "rescue" component of school choice. However, the second and larger aim is to induce systemic reform of the present system of public schools by means of competition from alternative education providers; this is defined as the "reform" component of school choice. Although all types of school choice have a rescue component, not all have a strong reform component.

While some school choice advocates have always preferred tax credits over vouchers, there has been a general shift of emphasis in recent years toward tax credits and away from vouchers. Vouchers are generally viewed as more controversial, difficult to pass, and subject to regulation. Tax credits, on the other hand, are generally viewed as carrying less baggage than vouchers since they do not involve the use or allocation of tax dollars, and therefore should be less subject to regulation. For example, in 2007, reform advocate John Stossel rejected vouchers in favor of tax credits,[8] and the following year Sol Stern penned a provocative article for *City Journal*, arguing that "School Choice Isn't Enough."[9] In Stern's view, vouchers have helped children get into better schools but they haven't produced the kind of reform of the public schools that he and others had been led to believe would occur. As a result, Stern now argues for backing other reforms such as instructional reform.

The current situation in the school choice arena is where a master chef—Milton Friedman—has come up with a school choice recipe that is good for cooking up a dynamic free market in K-12 education such that a variety of education providers vie for a share of the available school funds. Other chefs have taken this recipe, modified the ingredients to suit their own tastes and priorities, and claimed—or implied—that their modified recipes would still produce the same results as Friedman's. However, changing the recipe produces a different result from the outcome predicted by Friedman. Thus, we need to examine what are the essential ingredients in the creation of a free market in education.

Creation of a Free Market in K-12 Education

Friedman's 1955 voucher proposal was designed to create a competitive education marketplace. However, it is important to define the essential components of a free market in K-12 education so that the design of school choice programs is consistent with the objective of producing such a market. As Myron Lieberman noted in 2002, existing school choice programs do *not* create a free market in education. Instead, he said, they consist of "means-tested vouchers that exclude for-profit schools, severely restrict eligibility, are under constant threat of termination, are small scale in economic terms, and are subject to anti-competitive regulations of one kind or another."[10]

To create a competitive market, Friedman said the voucher should be available to all children, should be sufficient to pay for a good education at a private school, should not impose detailed regulations, should not prohibit parents from adding to the value of the voucher, and should be redeemable at for-profit, not-for-profit, and religious schools. Friedman also stressed the importance of including higher-income families in voucher programs in order to create the kind of market where innovation and experimentation would lead to quality improvement and cost savings. That's because such families are the early adopters of new developments and innovations.

"One function played by the rich is to finance innovation," explained Friedman. "They bought the initial cars and TVs at high prices and thereby supported production while the cost was being brought down, until what started out as a luxury good for the rich became a necessity for the poor."[11]

Another key element of an education market, according to economist John Merrifield in a recent Cato Institute report, is the stability of the program, so that producers have confidence in a projected revenue stream.[12] Merrifield also emphasized the need for low regulatory barriers to entry.

At a 2004 Cato Institute conference on "Creating a True Marketplace in Education," Lisa Snell of the Reason Foundation identified the following three requirements as essential for establishing a competitive free market in K-12 education:[13]

- First, and most important, is that the money follows the child. "There has to be competition for money."
- Second, funding must come from a stable revenue source and have sufficient purchasing power for companies to be interested in investing in new school capacity.
- Third, for-profit companies must be permitted to own and operate schools because for-profit companies are the only ones who will make the R&D investments necessary to develop specialized schools and be interested in replicating them.

The last two conditions are most important for producing a high level of participation by private schools. In addition, the K-12 education industry should be regulated only to the extent that is necessary for safety and nondiscrimination. While a low voucher value would largely limit private school participation to parochial schools, a higher voucher value would attract the interest of more private schools and educational entrepreneurs, but their actual participation would then depend on the level of the accompanying regulation.

Thus it appears that Friedman's original voucher proposal included almost all of the key elements necessary to create a vigorous free market in K-12 education: a well-funded voucher, redeemable at any approved school, available to all children, including those from wealthy families, with parents able to add on to the value of the voucher, and with minimum barriers to entry. The only component he neglected to identify was the need for a stable revenue source.

Assessment of the Efficacy of School Choice Programs

If the best school choice program design is the one that leads to a free market in education, which school choice programs are capable of achieving that objective? In systems engineering terms, Is the proposed system capable of achieving the objectives that have been established for it?[14] Milton Friedman's insistence on judging programs by their results rather than by their intentions is another way of asking the same question: We know where we want to get to, but can each of the different school choice programs get us there?

As noted above, as different varieties of school choice have developed, the focus has shifted from reforming public schools to rescuing children from failing public schools—with the implicit assumption that a rescue operation will also produce reform.[15] In fact, programs designed as rescue operations are being evaluated as if they were reform operations, and that's why many of these evaluations of school choice are failing to find significant reforms. The programs were never designed for reform in the first place, but are simply rescue operations.

Table 3.1 summarizes the different types of school choice program that have been established to date—public school choice programs, voucher programs, and tax-credit programs. These programs will be reviewed in turn, focusing primarily on how they differ in their capability of bringing about reform of the public school system. Each program is classified with regard to whether it meets one or both of two possible outcomes of a school choice program: rescue and reform. Every choice program is capable of rescuing children from failing schools—giving them a chance to transfer out—but the key question is, Does the program also produce systemic reform of the public school system?

1. Public School Choice

Public school choice is publicly funded choice involving only public schools. Although there are actually more types of choice in public schools than the ones listed in table 3.1—such as magnet schools and selective admission high schools—the three types listed are ones where the money follows the child to the school that is chosen by the child's parents. As explained earlier, the idea of the funding following the child is also an essential feature of voucher programs.

The first type of public school choice program is Open Enrollment, where—as in Minnesota—parents are permitted to choose public schools in other school districts and the per-pupil funding follows the child from the home district to the chosen district. However, the money generally does not follow the child to the receiving school but instead flows to the district.

The second type is Weighted Student Funding, a school choice reform that originated in the Edmonton School District in Canada, where it has been very successful.[16] Essentially, the way Weighted Student Funding works is this: each student is assigned a funding factor that is weighted according to the status of the student with regard to poverty, limited English proficiency, special education, and so on—that is, the student's relative degree of educational difficulty. The more difficult the child will be to educate, the more funding is assigned to that child. The weighted funds for the child then follow the child to the school the parents choose. This type of program is a school-district-level program, and a restricted version of Weighted Student Funding is in use in the Seattle, Houston, and San Francisco School districts.

The third type involves charter schools, where parents may choose a public school that is largely independent of the school district and run by an independent private organization. The funding for the child's education follows the child to the chosen school.

By and large, charter school development has been more focused on the creation of successful individual charter schools than on replicating success across multiple schools, the major exceptions being Knowledge is Power Program (KIPP) charter schools, National Heritage Academies, and Life Skills Centers. In addition, the education establishment has been very effective in lobbying state legislators to limit the growth of charter schools or to add operating requirements that stymie growth and expansion. Consequently, with the possible exception of post-Katrina New Orleans, where charter schools now make up three-quarters of the city's public schools, charter schools have not created much pressure on public schools to reform. Despite these limitations, there are some very innovative charter schools and, as Lisa Snell has noted, these schools provide an indication of what types of school would be possible if

Table 3.1 Types of school choice programs

	Program	Outcome 1: Rescue of students from failing schools	Outcome 2: Reform of the public school system	Religious schools included?	Comments
1. Public School Choice (education funds follow the child the chosen public school)	1.1 Open Enrollment (across districts)	Yes	Minimal	Not permitted	Reform effects are usually limited and localized.
	1.2 Weighted Student Funding (within district)	Yes	Some	Not permitted	Key is giving principals control over staffing and student-generated revenues at individual schools. The district teacher contract is a major barrier to implementing WSF.
	1.3 Charter Schools (usually within district)	Yes	Some	Not permitted	Reform effects are usually limited and localized. Charter schools draw an estimated 20 percent of their students from non-public schools.
2. Vouchers (education funds follow the child to the chosen private school)	2.1 "Charity" Vouchers (targeted programs)	Yes	Varies, but can be substantial	Yes, but optional	Reform effects depend on the size of the voucher and, while limited, these effects are usually sustainable. When the voucher value is low, religious schools predominate.
	2.2 Option-Demand Universal Vouchers (voucher is less than per-pupil public school spending)	Yes	Substantial, with a well-funded voucher	Yes, but optional	With a well-funded voucher, reform effects are likely to be substantial and sustainable since successful innovations in instruction and delivery would be quickly adopted by competing education providers. Caps would limit reform effects.

	Col 1	Col 2	Col 3	
2.3 Universal Vouchers (equal funding for all students in public and private schools)	Yes	Substantial	Yes, but optional	Reform effects are likely to be substantial and sustainable since successful innovations in instruction and delivery would be quickly adopted by competing education providers.
3. Tax Credits and Tax Rebates (reducing the cost of choosing a private school by means of tax code provisions)				
3.1 Individual Nonrefundable Tax Credits	Yes	Minimal to some, depending on type of credit and cap	Yes	Reform effects are likely to be minimal since state income tax credits are too low to attract new education providers; property tax credits would have a stronger reform effect but are likely to be capped at a low level.
3.2 Individual Refundable Tax Credits	Yes	Substantial, if the credit is large and uncapped	Yes	Reform effects would be substantial with a large refundable tax credit, but these credits are almost certain to be capped at a relatively modest level.
3.3 Scholarships Funded by Individual or Corporate Tax Credits	Yes	Minimal	Yes	Reform effects are likely to be limited because scholarship distribution is dispersed, not concentrated, and alternative education providers may not view projected revenue streams as being sufficiently reliable. Also, based on current programs, caps at a relatively low level are likely.
3.4 Individual Tax Rebates	Yes	Moderate, if the rebate is uncapped	Yes	Reform effects are likely to be moderate and concentrated in those public schools that experience the largest revenue loss from rebates. Caps would limit these effects.

the K-12 education market actually became "free."[17] Some examples of innovative charter schools are those noted above, the MATCH Charter School in Boston, Massachusetts, the BASIS charter schools in Arizona, and the Valley New School in Appleton, Wisconsin.

All three types of public school choice give parents a choice of schools and allow them to rescue their children from failing schools, but does public school choice spur failing public schools and underperforming districts to improve significantly? Does public school choice result in a level of competition that produces systemic reform? The answer has to be "No," even though some public school improvements have been observed as a result of public school choice. This is because almost all of the school choices available under public school choice are choices within the system. The situation is analogous to the choice of stores that were available to Soviet citizens living in the USSR under communism: There were different stores, but they were still all government stores, with the government deciding what kind of stores would open and how to stock them. Similarly, with public school choice, there are different schools available to parents—including many fine schools—but they are all still government schools with the government deciding what schools will open and what educational offerings will be made available in them.

2. Vouchers

There are essentially three types of voucher programs: targeted or "charity" vouchers, which are limited to a specific population group; John Merrifield's "option-demand universal vouchers," where the voucher value is less than the per-pupil spending in the public schools;[18] and "universal" vouchers of the kind envisioned by Milton Friedman in 1955. Friedman suggested a well-funded voucher, available to all children, redeemable at any approved school, with parents able to add on to the value of the voucher.

However, the voucher programs that have been created to date are not the universal type, but programs targeted to serve particular groups of students. Although these vouchers are funded at a relatively low level to begin with, parents still are not permitted to add on to the value of the voucher. As a result of this cap on tuition, the number of private schools interested in participating in such programs is limited. The interest of private schools is diminished even more by the fact that they are not allowed to set admission standards for their schools—unlike public schools, which are permitted to select students for magnet schools and to test students for admission to selective enrollment high schools.

Despite all these limitations, even charity vouchers appear capable of prompting reforms in the public schools. For example, a recent study of the Milwaukee Parental Choice Program shows that the availability of school choice has given school reformers sufficient clout to get the school district to provide more of the programs that parents want—such as Montessori schools and before and after school programs. It also appears to have prompted the district to reduce its dropout rate and improve the high school graduation rate, despite having to cope with an increasing percentage of low-income and minority students.[19] The gains have been particularly beneficial to minority students, with a significant reduction in the high school graduation gap between white and minority students.

Although these reforms are welcome, they still are not the kind of striking reforms that we would expect if there were a dynamic marketplace in K-12 education, driven by a well-funded voucher available to all children. When "school choice" means only having a choice of schools, it does appear that "school choice isn't enough," as Stern argued in his *City Journal* article. Merely having a choice of schools isn't enough to create vigorous competition for students. What would create such a marketplace would be vouchers like those proposed by Friedman in 1955—better-funded vouchers, vouchers that are available to more students, vouchers that parents can add on to, and vouchers that allow schools to set admission standards for their students.

3. Tax Credits

As explained earlier, this kind of school choice is fundamentally different in mechanism and intent from the previous two kinds, public school choice and vouchers. Public school choice and vouchers both work within the system of K-12 education funding that already exists and both aim to improve the performance of the system by changing the way that existing funds are allocated to schools. Both public school choice and vouchers are evolutionary developments in school finance—they work within the existing financial support structure while attempting to make the system more productive and more responsive to parents because of the competition for education dollars.

Tax credits, however, involve a quite different approach that brings new money into the K-12 education system. The intent of tax credits is to make it easier for parents to choose a nonpublic school by lowering the cost of making that choice with a tax credit against state income taxes. For example, in Illinois there is an education tax credit for 25 percent of education-related expenses up to a maximum credit of $500. Some 249,314 families made use of the credit in 2008.[20] However, the small amount of money involved per student is not enough to attract new and innovative education providers and create a dynamic marketplace in K-12 education. Individual nonrefundable tax credits help rescue children from failing schools, but their dollar value is much too low to prompt any significant competition among education providers.

On the other hand, nonrefundable tax credits do not, by law, involve the use of tax dollars. Thus, when private schools accept money derived from tax credits, no public funds are involved and so there is little justification for additional government regulation.

A question that arises with tax credits is, How do they help the poor, who are most in need of alternative schools but have little or no tax liability against which to take a credit? There are two ways of modifying tax credits so that they can help poor families pay for their children to be educated in private school.

One modification is to make the tax credit refundable. A refundable tax credit is similar to a reverse income tax. If the tax code provides for a refundable tax credit of $500 but a taxpayer pays zero state taxes, he or she would get a check (a "tax refund") for $500 from the state. In principle there is no reason why a refundable tax credit couldn't be for as much as the entire cost of private school tuition, making it similar to a voucher. However, many tax-credit advocates are opposed to refundable tax credits since the "refunds" must be paid for by an appropriation of tax dollars, which eliminates the "no public funds" advantage of tax credits over vouchers. Currently, Minnesota is the only state with a refundable tax credit—of up to $1,000 per child per family—but the average credit taken is less than $300.[21]

Another way of structuring tax credits to provide school choice for poor families is through a scholarship tax credit, where individuals and corporations receive a tax credit for donating funds to organizations that grant private school tuition scholarships to low-income families. These scholarships are often called "vouchers," which implies that they are publicly funded. A more accurate term would be "privately funded vouchers" since no public money is appropriated for them.

While tax-credit scholarships do succeed in rescuing children from failing schools, they are unlikely to create the vibrant free market in K-12 education that their advocates envision.[22] That's because any type of tax-credit program will almost certainly be capped in some way to limit the tax revenue loss to the state's coffers. Current programs, which have been implemented in several states, are capped at very low levels. For example, scholarships from the largest program, Arizona's Personal Tax Credit, average less than $2,000 per student and total less than 1 percent of the state's annual spending on K-12 education. At such low levels of funding, scholarship tax credits are unlikely to become a significant factor in reforming the public schools. This view is supported by the results of a recent study of Florida's Tax Credit Scholarship Program by Northwestern University researchers David Figlio and Cassandra Hart. They found that the competitive effect of the scholarships—currently worth $3,950 per student—does produce an improvement in public school test scores, but the size of the improvement is quite small.[23]

4. Tax Rebates

The final flavor of school choice is property tax rebates, which exist only in proposal form. Some tax-credit advocates have proposed credits against education-related property taxes but no such tax credit exists.[24] The advantage of using property taxes for credits and rebates is that they include low-income families, as described for education tax rebates in the 1988 book, *We Can Rescue Our Children*.[25] While many people pay too little in state income taxes to make an income tax credit amount to more than a small share of the cost of private school tuition, many do pay substantial amounts in property taxes to fund local government schools. Renters also pay property taxes via their rent, and their share of a building's property taxes can be readily calculated. As mentioned earlier, a key feature of a property tax rebate is that it involves parents directly in the allocation of some of their education tax dollars to private schools.

The advantage of a tax rebate over a tax credit is that a rebate is paid directly by the taxing authority to the applicant immediately after the taxes are paid, whereas funds from tax credits are available only after a tax return has been filed. The applicant can use the rebate funds right away for private school tuition, and the taxing authority—the local school district—also knows right away that it has lost property tax revenue to a private school. This rapid recognition of revenue losses is likely to enhance the competitive effect of property tax rebates relative to property tax credits.

Practical Considerations

The late Marquette University scholar Quentin Quade said that if a school choice program would move us in the direction of the "North Star"—Quade's term for universal vouchers—then we should embrace it, even if it's not perfect. While this is an appropriate standard by which to judge school choice proposals, there are some important issues to consider in the development of these proposals.

First, it should be clear what policy objective the proposal is built on—is it to offer parents an exit option to get their child out of the public schools, or is it to offer an exit option that also induces reform of the public schools? If it's the first, then any school choice program will suffice. However, only certain kinds of school choice programs are capable of achieving the second objective.

Second, the objective of a particular program should be framed in the context of the rationales for existing public programs. This is an easy matter since the essential features of school choice provide a strongly defensible public purpose for almost all school choice programs, such as increasing freedom, empowering parents by devolving decision-making authority to them, and strengthening communities by encouraging a diversity of schools.

Third, it is preferable for the choice program's funding to be drawn from the funds allocated for K-12 education since this would enhance competition. This is important where program caps are concerned, since the argument for raising the cap on a successful program is then simply one about a different allocation of funds that already are assigned to K-12 education.

Fourth, it's important to recognize that some obstacles are unlikely to be overcome in the near term. For example, even though the U.S. Supreme Court has ruled in *Zelman v. Simmons-Harris* (2002) that there is no constitutional bar to including religious schools in voucher programs, Andrew Coulson has pointed out that all but three state constitutions contain Blaine-type amendments or "compelled support" clauses that provide obvious grounds for legal challenges to vouchers.[26] Thus, a more prudent strategy might be to follow the example of Rep. Williams with the Milwaukee voucher program: First secure passage of a voucher program for secular schools only, and then, once that program has been established, work to expand it to include religious schools.

Proposed Design for a Comprehensive School Choice System

Just as one size does not fit all in public schooling, one size does not fit all in school choice. Parents need a variety of options to choose from, and it is not necessary to address the needs of all parents and children with a single school choice program. If different programs were designed to serve different purposes, parents would have a menu of educational options to choose from for their children. The following comprehensive school choice system, with both rescue and reform components, was designed to provide just such a menu that offers parents a full range of educational choices.

Menu Item #1: Public School Choice

Open enrollment would be available to permit school choice across school districts. Charter schools would also be authorized and individual public schools would be permitted to establish themselves as charter schools.

- These two provisions offer more choices for parents who want their children to remain in public schools, and they provide a means for public schools to respond to competition from other education providers.

- They also establish the public school equivalent of vouchers, where the funding follows the child to the school of choice.

Menu Item #2: An Individual Income Tax Credit for Educational Expenses

This nonrefundable credit would be applicable against state income taxes for any out-of-pocket educational expenses, such as books, tuition, and other fees.

- The rationale for this credit is that it supports parental educational efforts, including homeschooling.
- This credit also partially addresses the double-payment issue for parents who send their children to nonpublic schools.
- It also provides a means for private schools to respond to the loss of students to charter schools.

Menu Item #3: An Individual Property Tax Rebate

This rebate would be available to parents sending their children to religious or secular private schools and would be for the amount paid in local education-related property taxes.

- This rebate addresses the issue of parents who currently have to pay twice to educate their children when they are educated in a nonpublic school.
- The rebate would include renters, who pay property taxes via their rent.
- Other taxpayers and businesses would receive a rebate for a portion of their education-related property taxes if they made a donation to a private school or to a child's tuition expenses.

Menu Item #4: A Scholarship Tax Credit

This credit would be applicable against state income taxes and the resulting scholarships could be directed to religious or secular not-for-profit schools.

- This credit provides corporations and families with a way to support educational efforts in the community.

Menu Item #5: A School Voucher

The voucher would be available to all children and would be worth at least 75 percent of per-pupil public school spending; it would have an add-on option, be phased in by local public school performance (worst first), and be redeemable only at secular schools, both for profit and not-for-profit. Participating schools would be allowed to set admission criteria comparable with those applied in many public schools.

- The rationale for this voucher provision is that in a free society committed to educating the public at taxpayer expense, parents are entitled to choose an approved nongovernment school without financial penalty.
- If the tuition is lower than the voucher amount, the surplus may be placed in an Education Savings Account for later use for college tuition.
- If a student graduates a year or more early, half of the voucher amount for the unused year(s) may be used for college tuition.

Menu Item #6: A Special Education Voucher

This voucher would be directed to disabled students and would be available for the full amount of funding the child would have received in the public schools; it would have an add-on option and would be redeemable at religious schools as well as at secular for-profit and not-for-profit schools so as to provide as wide an array of treatments as possible for disabled students.

Performance Criteria

All individual choice schools must submit their students annually to at least two (year-beginning and year-ending) curriculum-based external tests of the school's choosing and publish the results on a timely basis; results must be published by cohort; high schools must publish dropout statistics, graduation statistics, job and college destination statistics, and subsequent four-year college graduation statistics.

Do School Choice Programs Inevitably
Lead to Excessive Regulation?

A major concern among school reformers is that vouchers would bring additional regulation to private schools and gradually result in private school autonomy being replaced by conformity with a wide range of government-established criteria and policies. Proponents of tax credits argue that these regulatory encroachments are much less likely with tax credits because tax credits do not involve the use of public money and therefore do not require the same public oversight as vouchers.

However, if education tax credits expand to the point where billions of dollars are involved, there would almost certainly be a strong push for additional regulation. There is no constitutional barrier to such regulation. According to the 1925 U.S. Supreme Court ruling in *Pierce v. Society of Sisters*, nonpublic schools can be regulated even if they do not receive public funds. Here's what the Court said:

> No question is raised concerning the power of the state to reasonably regulate all schools, to inspect, supervise, and examine them, their teachers and pupils, to require that all children of proper age attend some school, that teachers should be of good moral character and patriotic disposition, that certain studies plainly essential to good citizenship must be taught and that nothing be taught which is manifestly inimical to the public welfare.

Thus, it is clear that government can establish rules and regulations for private schools even if the schools do not make use of public money. As Quentin Quade stressed, avoiding the use of public money is not what holds off excessive government regulation but citizen vigilance.[27] But he also noted that legislative language can be very helpful, too, such as provisions in school choice laws that state, "There shall be no additional regulation of independent schools because of this legislation beyond what is already required in terms of health and safety rules." In model school voucher legislation developed for Illinois, Heartland Institute President Joseph Bast suggested legislative language stating that the preservation of private school autonomy is in the public interest, which protects all private schools from increased regulation, including those that do not participate in the school choice program.[28]

While some choice advocates may think their work is done when a program is enacted into law, school choice advocate Howard Fuller warned in 2001 that putting a program in place like the one in Milwaukee was only one stage of a multiphase battle against relentless "protectors of the status quo [who] are not just going to go quietly into the night."[29] Fighting off unnecessary regulations and countering misinformation about school choice are the last two phases of this long-term battle. There is no substitute for citizen vigilance and principled opposition to this persistent drumbeat for more regulation. However, Fuller, with the Black Alliance for Educational Options, and Susan Mitchell of School Choice Wisconsin, have successfully fought to keep the Milwaukee Parental Choice Program relatively free of additional regulation, and their continuing efforts provide a model for others to emulate.

Notes

1. Lewis Carroll, *Alice's Adventures in Wonderland* (1865).
2. G. M. Jenkins and P. V. Youle, *Systems Engineering: A Unifying Approach in Industry and Society*, Watts, London (1971).
3. Joel Spring, *The American School, 1642–1985*, Longman Inc., White Plains, NY (1986).
4. Ken Burns, "Interview with George Will," Public Broadcasting Corporation (undated). http://www.pbs.org/jefferson/archives/interviews/Will.htm.
5. Milton Friedman, "The Role of Government in Education," in *Economics and the Public Interest*, edited by Robert A. Solo, Rutgers University Press, 1955.
6. Krista Kafer, "A Chronology of School Choice in the U.S.," Policy Report IP-3-2007, Independence Institute, June 2008.
7. Herbert J. Walberg, Michael J. Bakalis, Joseph L. Bast, and Steven Baer, *We Can Rescue Our Children*, Green Hill Publishers, Ottawa, IL (1988).
8. John Stossel, "With Government Money Come Strings," TownHall.com, November 7, 2007. http://www.townhall.com/columnists/John Stossel/2007/11/07/with_government_money_come_strings.
9. Sol Stern, "School Choice Isn't Enough: Instructional Reform Is the Key to Better Schools," *City Journal*, Winter 2008. http://www.city-journal.org/2008/18_1_instructional_reform.html.
10. Myron Lieberman, "Voucher 'Experiments' Don't Test Competition," *School Reform News*, August 2002. http://www.heartland.org/Article.cfm?artId=1028.

11. Milton Friedman, "School Vouchers Turn 50," *The Insider*, Spring 2006. http://www.insideronline.org/archives/2006/spring/chap4.pdf. http://www.friedmanfoundation.org/friedman/newsroom/ShowArticle.do?id=15.
12. John Merrifield, "Dismal Science: The Shortcomings of U.S. School Choice Research and How to Address Them," Cato Institute, Policy Analysis No. 16, April 16, 2008.
13. George A. Clowes, "What Does It Take to Create a Marketplace in Education?" *School Reform News*, December 2004. http://www.heartland.org/publications/school%20reform/article.html?articleid=16047.
14. Jenkins and Youle (1971), supra, Note 2.
15. Current voucher and tax credit programs are summarized in "The ABCs of School Choice, 2011 Edition," The Foundation for Educational Choice, February 2011. http://www.edchoice.org/Foundation-Services/Publications/ABCs-of-School-Choice.aspx.
16. "Fund the Child: Tackling Inequity & Antiquity in School Finance," Policy Report, Thomas B. Fordham Institute, June 2006. http://www.eric.ed.gov/PDFS/ED495066.pdf.
17. Clowes (2004), supra, Note 13.
18. Merrifield (2008), supra, Note 12.
19. George A. Clowes, "Can Vouchers Reform Public Schools? Lessons from the Milwaukee Parental Choice Program," Heartland Institute Policy Study No. 120, July 2008. http://www.heartland.org/Article.cfm?artId=23538.
20. The Foundation for Educational Choice (2011), supra, Note 15.
21. Ibid.
22. Adam B. Schaeffer, "The Public Education Tax Credit," Cato Institute, Policy Analysis No. 6055, December 2007. http://www.cato.org/pubs/pas/pa-605.pdf.
23. David N. Figlio and Cassandra M. D. Hart, "Competitive Effects of Means-Tested School Vouchers," National Bureau of Economic Research, June 2010. http://www.nber.org/papers/w16056.
24. Schaeffer (2007), supra, Note 22.
25. Walberg et al. (1988), supra, Note 7.
26. Andrew Coulson, "Forging Consensus," Mackinac Center Report, April 2004. http://www.mackinac.org/archives/2004/s2004-01.pdf.
27. George A. Clowes, "Strap on the Armor and Go: Never Give In!" An Exclusive Interview with Quentin L. Quade, *School Reform News*, June 1998. http://www.heartland.org/Article.cfm?artId=12700.
28. Joseph L. Bast, "The Heartland Plan for Illinois: Model School Voucher Legislation," Policy Study No. 98, The Heartland Institute, May 2002. http://www.heartland.org/policybot/results/9492.
29. "Long Choice Struggle Ahead, Catholics Warned," *School Reform News*, June 2001. http://www.heartland.org/publications/school%20reform/article.html?articleid=957.

Chapter 4

Private Choice as a Progressive Disruptive Technology

Matthew Ladner

Achieving an Ideal Choice Program

Markets provide the highest-quality and most specialized goods and services at the lowest possible prices. Education is no exception to this rule. Currently, public policy badly skews and distorts this market in schooling, and the evidence of these distortions lies all around us.

Some make the argument that the only real solution to our education problems would be to return to a completely private, fee-for-service system. Such a proposal, making no allowance for equity issues, won't likely ever receive serious consideration. Hard-liner individualists may believe that people should live with the consequences of bringing children into the world, including educating them. Most, however, would see this as allowing the sins of the father, so to speak, to fall upon their children if society made no collective effort to provide an opportunity for children to be educated.

The goal should be to get as close as possible to the free market ideal while still addressing basic equity concerns. The question is not "Should we make a social effort to educate students from disadvantaged backgrounds?" We will attempt to do so. The question is "How to best achieve that goal with minimal distortion?"

The ideal choice system, to my mind, would include the following elements: robust parental choice, an emphasis on for-profit education, near universal fee payments by parents, provision of subsidy for disadvantaged children, transparency for results, and the lessening of the subsidy for the affluent.

Such a system would get as close to a pure market as we can realistically expect. Competition among schools would be fierce, and creative destruction would reward success and harshly sanction failure. Bad schools would suffer the same fate as bad restaurants. Someone providing high-quality and affordable schooling could make an attractive profit by driving less successful competitors out of the market. Government subsidies for disadvantaged children would introduce market distortions, but this would be a problem to manage.

None of this will be happening anytime soon. The more salient question is how to progress away from today's system, which is almost entirely opposite of this ideal. Children and taxpayers suffer from this status quo in terms of both abysmal student performance and record high inflation-adjusted spending per pupil.

I will argue below that the best way to proceed is for the movement to treat school choice as a "progressive disruptive technology." Choice advocates should seek programs that are as broad as they can achieve, but always advance the movement by creating programs to serve students who are particularly poorly served by the public school system. This strategy should emphasize equity issues and address them in private choice bill design. Private school choice will become much more widespread when it is recognized as a more effective and more just system for delivering education services.

Ideals and Realities of American K-12 Education

The ideals of American public schools are noble: universal education and access. The execution leaves much to be desired.

Reformers have made great efforts to improve K-12 education in recent years. The American form of government stresses incremental rather than revolutionary change. With separation of powers, checks and balances, and multiple veto points, defenders of the status quo generally have a strong advantage in defeating change. Throw in the huge size and scale of the forces interested in maintaining the status quo in education and the powerful hold that the ideals of public education (more than the realities) have on the public imagination, and radical change will be a long time in coming.

These political realities are obstacles to perfection, but not to progress. Nationally, nearly one-fourth of K-12 students now attend schools other than their zoned public schools, opting instead for an array of public and private options—open enrollment, magnet, charter, private, and home schools. And a large if unknown percentage of those children attending their zoned public school have purposely chosen their schools through the home-buying process.

Markets are the best way to provide the highest-quality goods and services at the lowest possible price. Little wonder, then, that American public schools, with third-party payers (the taxpayers) and zip-code-based assignment, often don't deliver a high-quality service and spend at record levels.

Nationwide, 34 percent of American fourth graders scored "below basic" in reading on the 2007 National Assessment of Educational Progress. Thus, more than a third of American fourth graders haven't learned to read in the critical early grades despite record spending by historical measures.[1] Enormous inequities exist in the public school system, some of which have only been revealed with the advent of value-added study of teacher quality. Inequities in teacher quality dwarf funding inequities in scale.

The way forward, I believe, is to move private choice programs forward as a disruptive technology, filling niches for students who are nonserved and served especially poorly in the current system. Along the way, there are a number of design flaws that advocates should be careful to avoid. The goal of this incremental process will be to build a body of evidence regarding the superiority of the approach with regard to both academics and equity. The ultimate goal should be to achieve a universal system of choice addressing legitimate equity concerns.

Private School Choice as a Disruptive Technology?

Clayton Christensen and his coauthors have made the case that online learning is a disruptive technology. Christensen describes a disruptive technology as competing against nonconsumption. A disruptive technology fills niches, serving as a more accessible product or service to those who otherwise would not be able to consume the product or service at all.

Eventually, through the course of normal incremental improvement, disruptive technology improves to the point where people recognize it to be superior to the dominant practice. After reaching this tipping point, the disruptive technology rapidly expands out of niches and into the mainstream.[2]

There is one large difference between the market examples provided by Christensen and his coauthors and the political enterprise of adopting parental choice: private choice almost always competes against demonstrable failure in the public system rather than nonavailability of schooling at all. Inner-city students in Cleveland, for example, have access to public schools. The problem isn't that they don't have access to schools at all; it is that the schools they do have access to often perform outrageously poorly. Thus we experience political difficulty in promoting private choice. It would be much easier to compete against nonconsumption.

Ironically enough, Democratic State Senator Royce West in Texas proposed just this sort of bill during the 2007 legislative session: a school voucher bill for dropouts. Senator West's bill did not make much progress in the 2007 Texas legislative session, and appears to be the first bill of its kind. The Texas Legislature did, however, create a High School Completion and Success Initiative Council that neared a vote on a plan to lower the state's dropout rate and improve the college and workforce readiness of high school graduates. This council created a dropout recovery program for dropouts including the participation of nonprofits—including private schools. The workings of this program remain unclear at the time of this writing, but the Texas teacher associations have filed suit against the Texas Education Agency to prevent the operation of what they describe as a voucher program.

Rita C. Haecker, president of the Texas State Teacher Association, told the *Dallas Morning News*, "they couldn't push vouchers through the Legislature in an above-board way, so they went through the back door to divert public dollars to private school programs."[3] The Christensen model might suggest that it would be a good idea to pursue voucher bills for dropouts, as it is easier to compete against nonconsumption.

Preschool vouchers represent another excellent example of voucher programs that have competed against nonconsumption. A large set of private preschools exist, and public schools often don't have space for expanded preschool programs. Accordingly, vouchers for preschool programs are both common and noncontroversial.

School Choice Mostly Serves the Poorly Served Rather Than Nonconsumers

The school choice movement, rather than targeting nonconsumers, has primarily although not exclusively sought to aid students poorly served by the public school system. Thus, the school choice movement experiences ferocious resistance from those interested in continuing to serve those students, however poorly. I would not expect this to change, nor should that struggle be abandoned.

The modern choice movement began in Milwaukee in 1990 when a group of frustrated inner-city Milwaukee Democrats teamed with Republican Governor Tommy Thompson to create the Milwaukee Parental Choice Program benefiting low-income students in Milwaukee.

Since that initial victory, we've seen the creation of Milwaukee-like programs in Cleveland and Washington DC, and failing school vouchers in Louisiana, Ohio, and Florida. Lawmakers have created broad eligibility tax-credit programs in Arizona, Illinois, and Georgia, and means-tested tax-credit programs in Arizona, Florida, Iowa, Minnesota, Pennsylvania, and Rhode Island. Voucher programs for children with disabilities have been passed in Arizona, Florida, Georgia, Ohio, and Utah, and Arizona passed the nation's first and (as yet) only voucher program for foster care children.

Some in the private choice movement would look at this list and say the movement needs to refocus on inner-city programs. Some in the choice movement have expressed discomfort about the success of the special needs programs. These sentiments reflect deeply held value preferences and beliefs about strategy. They are neither right nor wrong, but more a matter of perspective.

For reasons I will explain below, I very much disagree with such sentiments.

Hoisting the Status Quo on John Rawls' Petard

Matthew Miller's book *The 2% Solution* utilizes the philosophy of John Rawls to make the case for parental choice in education. Classical liberals (rightly in my view) raise objections to Rawls, and make the case that the philosophy of Rawls has been used as a justification for the government status quo. However, Matthew Miller, a progressive in good standing, provokes an interesting thought experiment by judging the status quo against Rawlsian ideals, and making the case for parental choice based upon it.

John Rawls' hugely influential work *A Theory of Justice* argued that societal ethics ought to be decided as if we were behind a theoretical "veil of ignorance." Behind the veil, no one would be aware of what his or her position would be in a forthcoming society. You would not know whether you would grow up the child of a billionaire or poor in the inner city. The veil creates an incentive to leave a path out of the latter scenario. While many contest Rawls' philosophy, it is hugely influential in left of center thinking. Does today's system of public education remotely approach the Rawlsian ideal?[4]

No, not even close. In fact, today's public education system closely resembles the opposite. Today's system in fact systematically disadvantages the poor.

Consider the expanding body of research on teacher quality. Researchers have shown that the effectiveness of individual teachers plays a huge role in student learning gains. Examining test scores on a value-added basis (looking at year-to-year gains) has revealed that some teachers are hugely effective, while others are much less so.

What we have not had before is quantifiable evidence regarding just how important high-quality teachers are in driving outcomes. Researchers examined the differences between teachers succeeding in adding value (the top 20 percent of teachers) and the least successful teachers (the bottom 20 percent). A student learning from low-quality teachers learns 50 percent less than a similar student learning from effective teachers during the same three-year period.[5]

The question then quickly becomes, how do we get more high-quality teachers into the classroom? Or, more to the point when discussing parental choice, how do we give children access to high quality teachers with empty seats in private schools? The entire private choice movement can be seen through the lens of increasing the pool of teachers from which parents can choose.

We can only accomplish this by making big systemic changes. Teaching is a profession with many rewards, but which has been tragically divorced from any recognition of merit. The teacher who works effectively and tirelessly is paid according to a salary schedule that will treat him or her identically to someone who does neither.

Job security and summers off are not big lures for the capable and ambitious sorts of people we need to attract into teaching in droves. To be sure, we have such people in our teaching ranks now, but the system treats them poorly. Our public schools do not pay them according to productivity—no rewards for success, no sanctions for failure. In short, we treat teachers not as professionals, but as unionized factory workers.

Most of our capable teachers will leave the profession frustrated, or go into administration. Those that we do keep in the classroom cluster in leafy suburbs far from the children who need them most.

What does the public system do for those children who lose in the Rawls lottery, who find themselves growing up in poor urban school districts? All too often, it assigns them to schools with decades-long histories of academic failure. These children will serially suffer ineffective instructors.

Frighteningly high percentages of these students will not learn to read at a developmentally appropriate age. Many will never learn to read. Such students fall further and further behind each year. Unable to read their textbooks, never envisioning themselves advancing on to higher education, they will begin to drop out in large numbers in late middle school.

Fortunately, it is not hard to envision a better system. Public schools today are spending beyond the dreams of avarice for administrators from previous decades. We simply need to get a much better bang for our buck. A captive audience of students promotes adult dysfunction in our schools. We should radically expand parental choice options, especially for disadvantaged students.

Our methods of hiring and compensating teachers today largely reflect the preferences of the education unions. The education unions oppose parental choice, merit pay for teachers, alternative certification, or differential pay based on teacher shortages. All of these positions are rational for a union boss but detrimental to children.

Of course, libertarians offer their own devastating critique of the status quo of the public school system, but the progressive case against it is also powerful. Can anyone who takes Rawlsian ideals seriously truly argue that a life lottery loser, say a low-income child born in inner-city Detroit, has the system of schooling that one would choose from the original position behind the veil of ignorance? Obviously not.

Getting back to Christensen's disruptive technology model, when can private school choice move beyond small programs and filling education niches? What will happen if parental choice is recognized as a superior technology in delivering education services than the dominant K-12 paradigm? If that moment comes, I believe it will not be solely based upon recognition of superior test scores, parental satisfaction, or taxpayer return on investment. Such factors will be necessary but not sufficient.

A key factor will also be that private choice is recognized as a more effective and thus a more *fair* system for educating children. Equality of opportunity is an extremely widely held value in America, and promoting it will be key to building support outside of philosophical libertarians and conservatives.

Bringing the Progressive Choice Movement beyond the Inner City

The zeal of the progressive private choice movement is to provide the opportunity for low-income inner-city children to attend a high-quality school. This is a passion I share, obsessively. Low-income inner-city children are too often trapped in schools so dysfunctional that no one reading this would consider having their own children attend them. The John Rawls criterion of justice is, if those schools aren't good enough for your children in theory, then they aren't good enough for disadvantaged children in practice.

Children with disabilities, however, have an equally compelling case for choice, and may in fact be the most poorly served children (with the most frustrated parents) in the public school system. Pop quiz: would you rather be born to a low-income family in an inner city or the son of a billionaire with autism? Personally, I'd choose to take my chances with the inner city.

The current IDEA system promises an "Individualized Education Plan" for children with disabilities, but all too often involves simply filing out the paperwork to prevent a successful lawsuit. Children—especially minority children—are often mistakenly shunted into special education due to poor reading instruction and effectively if not purposely left to rot academically in the most blatant and vivid example of the bigotry of low expectations imaginable.

The case for foster children is also compelling. Having already rolled snake-eyes in their opening roll in life, children in foster care bounce from home to home, and thus, because of attendance boundaries, from school to school. Ultrafrequent transfers between schools effectively destroy any chance they have to make academic progress.

Thinking again of the disruptive technology model: inner-city poor children are a niche we should seek to aid through parental choice. They do not, however, constitute the entirety of students extremely poorly served by the public school system. Inner-city children, children in failing schools, dropouts, English-language learners, foster care children, free and reduced lunch children, functional illiterates, and special needs children are all demonstrably poorly served in the public school system.

Research from Florida shows a positive impact of the McKay program for children with disabilities remaining in the public schools.[6] The same is true of the failing school program. Don't get me wrong: I prefer larger and broader programs to smaller ones. I'm most interested in helping as many poorly served children get as much access to a broad array of school choices as fast as possible, and building acceptance and evidence for choice in the process.

The passage of special needs bills was followed by choice bills with a broader set of eligibility criteria in both Utah and Georgia. From a disruptive technology perspective, that is a good thing and to be expected.

Viewed from the disruptive technology perspective, one could offer the (mild) criticism of the Wisconsin choice effort concerning the lack of having moved on to aid other niches of disadvantaged children. There are low-income children in places like Racine, for example, moving through dropout factory schools. Children with disabilities around the state could benefit enormously from a special needs voucher bill.

Ohio, on the other hand, started with a means-tested bill focused on Cleveland, and then moved on to a bill for children with autism and a statewide failing schools bill. Choice efforts in the state now focus on moving to a full-blown McKay bill.

Florida's programs focused on free and reduced lunch-eligible children (Step Up for Students Tax Credit), special needs students (McKay Scholarship Program), and students in failing schools (Opportunity Scholarships). That's a good start to build on, and Florida has overcome a very contentious debate on choice to develop bipartisan support and strong statewide public school improvement.

Special Needs as a Disruptive Opportunity

Daniel McGroarty outlined examples of inner-city voucher students in Milwaukee and Cleveland who had transferred to private schools using vouchers.[7] The maximum amount of those vouchers wasn't any different from that for children without disabilities. For children with mild (or sometimes in reality nonexistent disabilities) private schools may be able to accommodate such students, as will be discussed below. Ohio and Wisconsin lawmakers have chosen not to include additional funding for special needs students in their vouchers. This amounts to an opportunity for improvement in bill design.

Congress passed the Education of All Handicapped Children Act in 1975, which was renamed the Individuals with Disabilities Education Act (IDEA) in 1990. Congress passed this landmark legislation to prevent the then-widespread discrimination against children with disabilities by guaranteeing a "free appropriate public education" to children with disabilities. Nationwide, more than 13 percent of students in public schools are in special education programs, and the percentage continues to grow.

In 2001, the Thomas B. Fordham Foundation and the Progressive Policy Institute published an edited volume on the functioning of IDEA. This volume broke something of a taboo against criticizing IDEA by exposing a legion of problems with special education. These problems included but were not limited to the fact that IDEA emphasizes procedure over student achievement, that an alarmingly large number of children have been inappropriately placed in special education due to poor early reading instruction, and that there exists a racial bias in placement of minority children.

Growth in special education has made IDEA simultaneously costly and ineffective. By some estimates, 40 percent of the increase in K-12 spending has gone into special education. Special education, in short, does too little to help children with disabilities and too much to harm children without disabilities. Jay Mathews of the *Washington Post* noted that the available research "suggests that the special education system has led to widespread, if well-intentioned, misuse of tax dollars and has failed to help kids."

The McKay Scholarship Program for Students with Disabilities represents a radical departure from the normal operation of the special education system. McKay makes a school voucher available to any special education student in Florida public schools. This program is the largest school voucher program in the country, with approximately 375,000 eligible special education students and more than 21,000 students participating.

Students with an individual education plan (IEP) enrolled in a Florida public school are eligible to participate. Private schools meeting minimal requirements, including financial soundness and compliance with nondiscrimination regulations, can participate in the program. The maximum amount of each student's voucher is equal to the total cost of educating that child in public school.

Children in special education programs are disproportionately poor. Schools enroll poor and minority students into special education programs at higher rates than the general student population.[8]

Many people have a view of children with disabilities as children with obvious handicaps: blindness, mental retardation, and so on. In fact, the vast majority of the growth of special education has been the large increase of students classified as "learning disabled" (LD). School districts often label children as LD when teachers perceive a discrepancy between classroom performance and innate intellectual ability. Such a vague standard is subject to error and abuse. Students with learning disabilities constituted only 21 percent of all special education disabilities when Congress passed the Education for All Handicapped Children Act (EAHCA), but by 1998 that figure had more than doubled to 46 percent. While the number of students with clinical disabilities (such as autism, blindness, deafness, or mental retardation) has remained nearly constant since 1976, the percentage of all students classified as LD has more than tripled— from 1.8 percent of all students to 6 percent.

The McKay program required an early legislative tweak to prevent school district gaming of the system by changing the disability designation of students on their way out to transfer. Otherwise, the operation of the program has been smooth. The McKay program serves the largest number of students and has the largest funded eligibility pool of any choice program in the nation.

Almost 21,000 children participated during the 2009–10 school year, attending 959 private schools. The program delivered over $138,000,000 in aid to students that year.

Philanthropic resources devoted to the McKay program have been smaller than those to other smaller programs. While it would be an exaggeration to describe the McKay program as an elegant, self-executing program, it would certainly come closer to that ideal than other choice programs.

Funding should follow the child. Some care must be taken in the design of bill not to force private schools to take children they aren't equipped to deal with. The bill needs to be an opt-out of the public system for special needs children that does not bring red tape into the private school setting. The McKay statute effectively deals with both of these issues.

Accordingly, choice coalition members should include additional funding for special needs children if possible. Judge special education by the Rawls standard—is this the program you would want if you might be born as either a student with a disability or someone who might be mistaken for one? The status quo clearly flunks miserably. Once McKay-style programs are recognized as a highly effective and equitable reform of the status quo, they can proliferate across the country. In fact, this process has already begun.

Design Flaws to Avoid in Choice Programs

A Non-Deal-Breaker: Means Testing

I would divide design flaws in choice programs into two categories: deal-breakers and non-deal-breakers. These are purely a matter of personal preference. Let's start with non-deal-breakers.

First, means testing of choice programs falls into the category of a non-deal-breaking design flaw in my book. In essence, a school choice coalition should be willing to accept a means-tested bill if necessary, but should not be seeking it if they can avoid it.

Milton Friedman once said that programs for the poor are poor programs. I don't entirely agree, but there can be no doubt that Dr. Friedman was onto something important. Consider the ongoing example of Milwaukee Democrats continuing to vote to destroy the Milwaukee Parental Choice Program year after year despite having 18,000 children benefiting from the program.

Why do they do so? In part, they do so because they can get away with it. The income threshold for Milwaukee has been set to such a low level that many parents with children in the program do not vote or otherwise routinely engage in civic activities.

Choice advocates have developed a broad, although not universal, consensus to means test at higher income levels. This is a welcome development. We should ask, however, whether it is wise to means test at all, so long as we can address equity concerns in other ways.

Utah's universal voucher program is an elegant way forward: provide universal eligibility, but with a sliding scale giving larger amounts of financial assistance to lower-income children. My advice would be—pass a means-tested bill if you must, avoid it if you can, but take equity issues seriously.

A Deal-Breaker:
State Standards Testing of Students

School choice is about promoting a diversity of options for parents. It begins with the premise that there is no "one true way" to educate children, but that parents should be able to match their children with the best school to meet the individual needs of their child. Competition for students will create a process whereby success is rewarded, failure discarded.

One overriding concern for choice advocates must therefore be to always protect the independence of private schools. Charles Glenn's book *The Ambiguous Embrace* lays out the case for a greater option to attend private schools, but details the chilling result in some European countries, where, for instance, Catholic schools now essentially function as state schools that happen to include religious instruction.

Homogenization of private schools must be avoided. Fortunately, experience shows that it can be avoided in both voucher and tax-credit programs. The need for private school autonomy, however, must be balanced against the political desire for transparency and/or "accountability" to public agencies.

A delicate balance must be struck. Some in the choice movement believe that because tax-credit programs do not use "public funds" they can shield private schools from the need for transparency or "accountability." Perhaps this is the case, but it should be noted that states can and do routinely regulate private schools whether they are involved in choice programs or not. Others argue that even if tax-credit funds represent foregone public funds rather than public funds, a certain level of transparency is reasonable in return for the state foregoing the funds.

Private school participation in choice programs is always voluntary, mitigating if not eliminating the danger of state absorption. If state regulation becomes excessively onerous, then private schools can opt not to participate.

The bottom line is that the price of liberty is constant vigilance. Private schools need to mobilize to protect their independence even without a choice program in place, and must simply do so more in the event of a choice bill passing. Private schools in different states will have different preferences concerning how to balance autonomy and transparency.

One absolute stone-cold deal-breaker to my mind, however, is a requirement for student testing that mandates use of the state accountability test. This is a line in the sand; kill the bill before you accept such a provision. State accountability tests align with state curricula. This alignment would put pressure on private schools to align their curricula to state standards, fundamentally undermining the diversity available under choice.

I believe that choice supporters should view this point as non-negotiable in bill design. Further, they should be willing to "pull the plug" on an operating choice program rather than watch it morph into a parody of itself over time. The public has an interest in transparency (explained below) but choice advocates must maintain the independence of private schools at all cost.

Important Features to Include

1. Academic Transparency

If choice programs are ever to achieve widespread recognition as an effective and equitable method for delivering education services, they will need greater transparency than that currently delivered by many choice programs. This may appear to contradict what was written above concerning state testing, but in fact it does not.

Higher education serves as a chilling cautionary tale of what can go wrong with government-subsidized education delivery in a system with little transparency. Higher education costs have exploded with no evidence of increased quality.

Markets need transparency in order to function optimally. Student testing data should be made readily available for participating schools. Politically, legislators require reassurance that bad apples will be revealed. More broadly, the choice movement requires evidence of effectiveness.

Lawmakers can strike a reasonable balance between the need for private school independence, and the need for transparency lies in requiring schools to give participating students a national norm-referenced exam and to make the results public and accessible. If possible, these results should include value-added information.

Florida serves as an excellent best-practice example. Participating children must now take a national norm-referenced test or the state accountability exam. Results of these tests must be provided to both parents, and to an evaluator selected by the Florida Department of Education. The Florida Department of Education selected a scholar at the University of Florida to conduct the evaluation, and a first year baseline score analysis has been produced.

2. Financial Accountability

Making millions of dollars in public funds, or foregone public funds in the case of tax credits, available to private entities without adequate oversight can be a recipe for disaster.

Florida's accountability bill, passed in 2006, serves as a model for consideration throughout the choice movement. Encompassing both fiscal and academic accountability, it might be a difficult sell for private schools in many states absent the sort of beating Florida's programs took in the press before 2006. Anyone interested in an ounce of prevention rather than an emergency pound of cure, however, should examine the bill closely.

Having suffered through the controversy generated by two school funding organizations closing under a financial cloud, Florida choice advocates pushed a financial accountability bill. The law included several requirements for tax-credit student funding organizations (SFOs) and participating private schools. The bill required that SFO directors have no arrests and submit to fingerprinting and a level two background check. SFOs must now have separate accounts for administrative and scholarship funds. SFOs must send copies of an annual audit to the Florida Department of Education. In addition, SFOs must provide the Department of Education with student enrollment data and scholarship amounts. Student social security numbers must be provided in order to ensure that students aren't dual enrolled in public and private schools.

The accountability bill requires participating private schools to have been in operation for three years, or else to post a surety bond equal to half of the amount of the value of scholarships received. Participating schools must also produce a signed compliance form attesting that they have had all the inspections necessary under Florida law for private schools. School officials must sign and notarize the forms, and each year the Florida Department of Education reviews a third of all forms, requiring schools to produce evidence of the inspections.

Experience has shown that financial incompetence tends to be highly correlated with academic incompetence. The interests of the choice movement can therefore be doubly served by removing bad actors from choice programs.

Focusing on Equity Niches, Transparency, and Financial Accountability: Florida

Florida choice advocates have focused on three student niches self-evidently poorly served by the public schools: students with disabilities (McKay Scholarships), free and reduced lunch students (Step Up For Students Tax Credit), and students in failing public schools (Opportunity Scholarships). The private choice issue has been framed as an equality of opportunity issue.

Parental choice became a very contentious debate after the 1999 legislative session. The debacle of the 2000 recount battle certainly created a highly charged partisan atmosphere in the state. Jeb Bush's focus on education reform drew a fierce push-back from those seeking to defend the status quo. Finding fault or scandal with the choice programs, therefore, became a method for attacking and discrediting the governor.

In 2006, the Florida Supreme Court ruled the Opportunity Scholarship Program unconstitutional. The convoluted decision left unresolved whether the McKay Scholarship and Step Up for Students Programs would survive the legal challenge. Matters looked grim.

By May of 2008, however, choice advocates had turned things around. On the final day of the 2008 legislative session, Florida lawmakers passed an extremely robust improvement to the Step Up for Students tax credit. Lawmakers increased the cap on the program by $30 million per year, from $88 million to $118 million. In 2010, the Florida legislature increased the cap again, and set it to automatically increase when reached in the future.

SFOs that have been in operation for three or more years without scandal can now use up to 3 percent of funds to administer the program. The administrative allowance will free Florida choice advocates from the burden of having to raise millions of dollars to administer the Step Up for Students program.

Most exciting of all is that this bill got passed with substantial support from legislative Democrats. Almost half of the joint Florida House and the senate African American caucus voted for the expansion bill. The entire Hispanic caucus voted for the bill.

In 2006, Florida choice advocates had lost one of their programs and faced unrelenting hostility. In 2008, they passed a historic expansion with bipartisan support. A key to the change in those two years: the passage of an accountability bill for the Step Up for Students program. Florida has the most students participating in private choice programs, and has gone through the political storms to achieve bipartisan support.

Although the ability to utilize the voucher mechanism remains up in the air, the ability to make further progress on serving disadvantaged children seems to be a long-term possibility. If the evaluation on Step Up for Students shows strong results, then the natural question will be, how can we make this program larger and more effective? Only a fraction of low-income Florida children actually have an opportunity to utilize choice under the program due to limited funds. One could imagine introducing new taxes to credit or converting the entire program into a voucher to provide actual funded eligibility for the low-income children.

The evidence on McKay Scholarships thus far shows extremely high parental satisfaction rates and positive impact on the scores of disabled students in public schools.[9] Given such success, why not explore creating similar programs for English-language learners?

In 2005–06, Florida had just over 2.6 million public school students. Free and reduced lunch students, special needs students, and English-language learners added up to over 1.9 million students. Although the actual number of students eligible for choice under these categories alone is well below the 1.9 million figure (because many special needs students and English-language learners are also free and reduced lunch eligible), more than 1.2 million students qualified for free or reduced lunch alone.

Should Florida seek only to aid these disadvantaged students? I would certainly strike a bargain to stop at aiding disadvantaged students if that were the only way to bring aid to them. The ideal, however, would be a sliding scale system with variable funding for special education, English-language learners (temporarily), and low family income. Ideally, everyone should have access to such a system. I would argue, however, that none of these scholarships should ever pay the full cost of attending private school, and they should include reasonable measures for academic transparency.

Conclusion: Progress toward the Ideals of Choice Depends upon Equity and Effectiveness

The increasing willingness of elected Democrats to permit and at times even sponsor private parental choice bills in recent years demonstrates that a consensus can be struck for the right types of legislation. Democrats played leading roles in the creation and expansion of school choice bills in Florida, Iowa, Pennsylvania, and Rhode Island in recent years. Arizona Governor Janet Napolitano signed and/or permitted into law five different private choice measures during the 2005 and 2006 sessions. Pennsylvania Governor Ed Rendell has signed increases and improvements to the Education Improvement Tax Credit. The overwhelmingly Democratic Rhode Island legislature created a tax credit, and Democrats played a leading role in the Iowa effort as well.

Sadly, the education unions will fight such programs every step of the way. But progress can be made by focusing on equity issues. The focus of the movement should be on helping those who need it most, and building the case for effectiveness through transparency.

Notes

1. National Center for Education Statistics, National Assessment of Educational Progress, 2007, Fourth Grade Reading, available on the internet at http://nces.ed.gov/nationsreportcard/states/.

2. Chrisensen, Clayton, Michael B. Horn, and Curtis W. Johnson. 2008. *Disrupting Class: How Disruptive Innovation Will Change the Way the World Learns.* New York: McGraw Hill.

3. See Stutz, Terrence. 2008. "State Teacher Group Sues Texas Education Agency over Dropout-Prevention Vouchers Given to Nonprofits." Story appeared in the August 6, 2008, edition of the Dallas Morning News, available on the internet at http://www.redorbit.com/news/education/1513048/state_teacher_group_sues_texas_education_agency_over_dropoutprevention_vouchers/index.html.

4. Matthew Miller. 2003. *The Two Percent Solution: Fixing America's Problems in Ways Liberals and Conservatives Can Love.* Cambridge: Public Affairs.

5. Sanders, William L. and Sandra P. Horn Research Findings from the Tennessee Value-Added Assessment System (TVAAS) Database: Implications for Educational Evaluation and Research. Journal of Personnel Evaluation in Education 12:3 247-256. Available on the internet at http://www.sas.com/govedu/edu/ed_eval.pdf.

6. Jay Greene and Marcus Winters. 2008. The Effect of Special Education Vouchers on Public School Achievement: Evidence from Florida's McKay Scholarship Program. Manhattan Institute Civic Report Number 52, April 2008. Available on the internet at http://www.manhattan-institute.org/html/cr_52.htm.

7. McGroatry, Daniel. 2001. "The Little Known Case of America's Largest School Choice Program" in Chester E. Finn, Andrew Rotherham and Charles Hokanson (eds.) *Rethinking Special Education for a New Century.* Fordham Foundation report available on the internet at http://www.ppionline.org/ppi_ci.cfm?knlgAreaID=110&subsecID=900030&contentID=3344.

8. See Alfredo Artiles, et. al., "Over-Identification of Students of Color in Special Education: A Critical Overview," National Technical Assistance Center for Personnel Preparation in Special Education at Minority Institutions of Higher Education, 2001, available on the internet at http://www .monarchcenter.org/pdfs/overidentification.pdf.

9. See Greene, Jay P. and Marcus Winters. 2008. *The Effect of Special Education Vouchers on Public School Achievement: Evidence From Florida's McKay Scholarship Program,* Manhattan Institute Civic Report 52, available on the internet at http://www.manhattan-institute .org/html/cr_52.htm, and Greene, Jay P. and Greg Forster. 2003. *Vouchers for Special Education Students: An Evaluation of Florida's McKay Scholarship Program.* Manhattan Institute Civic Report 38, available on the internet at http://www.manhattan-institute .org/html/cr_38.htm.

Chapter 5

"Unbounded Liberty, and Even Caprice": Why "School Choice" Is Dangerous to Education

Sheldon Richman

Now, of all arts, those stand the fairest chance of being brought to perfection, in which there is opportunity of making the most experiments and trials.

Joseph Priestley (1733–1804)[1]

Introduction

Any government-administered "school choice" program would necessarily interfere with the private-school market—and *any* interference is excessive if our objective is the best possible educational environment.[2] The reasons for these contentions lie in the nature of democratic government and the nature of entrepreneurship in the marketplace. If a fully competitive educational market is desirable, it is imperative that the state not be permitted to meddle with either the supply or demand side of the market process. Only then will real school choice be available to parents and their children.

Fully competitive markets are indispensable to human progress because, among other reasons, our knowledge at any time is limited. We endure what the economist Israel Kirzner calls genuine error, or "utter ignorance" (in contrast to "rational ignorance")—that is, *unchosen, uncalculated* ignorance of information we would find useful in achieving our objectives if only we knew it was there to be grasped.[3]

The genius of competitive markets is that they, unlike planned economies, contain incentives to dispel utter ignorance. But if they are to do so, certain conditions must be met. These can be summed up in the phrase "complete freedom for suppliers and demanders." If markets are to do their job, government must not constrain them (beyond outlawing force and fraud); that is, it must not impose restraints on buyers and sellers (entrepreneurs) or otherwise interpose itself between them. To the extent it does, an unknown—and unknowable—array of options will never be offered by sellers to buyers. Consumers will be deprived of useful knowledge, products, and services, just as entrepreneurs will be deprived of profit opportunities. Gains from trade that would have occurred will never materialize. Market participants will thereby be worse off than they would have been in a free environment.[4]

Thus an optimal education market requires that political authorities not constrain entrepreneurs and parents in their peaceful pursuits. The policies known as "school choice"—that is, vouchers, tax credits, and charter schools—will inevitably entail some degree of constraint, making the educational "system" less than optimal. For education to be the best it can be, full freedom is necessary. For that reason, the free market is better than "school choice." Further, for reasons that will be discussed below, government-administered "school choice" plans may be seen as a step away from the free market, rather than a step in the right direction.

What Do We Want from Education?

Before we can answer the question, "can a school-choice program be designed without causing excessive interference with the private-school market?" we should be clear about the ultimate educational objective. Only then can we understand what would constitute interference.

One could go on at length describing the most desirable education "system,"[5] but it might best be summed up by saying it is a process that prepares children to live as self-directed, self-responsible adults in a free society. (Today schools appear intended to prepare children for life in an authoritarian society.) "Free society" for our purposes denotes the classical liberal, or libertarian, vision of the proper human community in which individuals freely cooperate and compete in peace to achieve the good life as each understands it. It includes not only the narrow set of civil liberties that enjoy wide support, such as freedom of speech, press, religion, and assembly, but also freedom justly to acquire, use, and dispose of property, beginning with land, and the freedom to trade property for mutual benefit. In other words, the free market is an intrinsic part, though not the entirety, of the free society.

Persons are most fully human when they are capable of exercising their intellectual and moral faculties to the fullest extent of their capabilities, that is, when they have sound notions of just conduct (respect for the freedom of others) and the ability to think for themselves. Training in those faculties is therefore among the most important responsibilities parents have toward their children. Hence, a proper educational environment is one that maximizes the chances that children will encounter educational experiences that will train them to reason and to live according to proper rules of just conduct. To be sure, imparting particular knowledge would be an important part of a good educational environment, but such teaching would occur within the larger context of encouraging the development of self-directed persons.

Historically, the proponents of state-run education have had other purposes in mind, such as molding "good citizens" who would be prepared to assume the roles of good soldiers, bureaucrats, and industrial workers.[6] In such a system, critical, independent thought is not prized, which is why individualist observers such as John Stuart Mill and H. L. Mencken recognized that government's priority in education was to impose uniformity on children. As Mill wrote in *On Liberty*, "a general State education is a mere contrivance for molding people to be exactly like one another." And Mencken, in *A Mencken Chrestomathy*, wrote, "the teaching process['s] . . . sole purpose is to . . . make the pupil a good citizen, which is to say, a citizen differing at little as possible, in positive knowledge and habits of mind, from all other citizens."[7]

Individuals differ across a wide range of traits—physical and mental. No two people are alike.[8] This complicates the objectives of any educational effort because children will respond differently to different methods of teaching. In judging which arrangement is best, account must be taken of the uniqueness of individuals. Given human differentiation, there is no reason to believe there is "one best system" suitable for all children.[9]

Education in an Open-Ended World

To live, human beings must act. All action is future oriented; some amount of time must pass between an action's inception and its completion. Yet human beings are plagued by ignorance. The future is necessarily uncertain. No one can know everything that will occur between the commencement and conclusion of a course of action. Everyone necessarily acts with incomplete and imperfect knowledge and in the face of a future shrouded in fog. Yet act we must—with the knowledge that one might discover tomorrow something that would have been highly useful yesterday.

One way we grapple with this uncertainty is market entrepreneurship. While all action is entrepreneurial in the sense that it entails risk in substituting a (subjectively conceived) more satisfactory condition for a less satisfactory condition, the marketplace is an arena in which professional entrepreneurs drive production of goods and services. These are individuals who seek profits by rearranging the use of scarce resources so that they more fully satisfy consumers according to their subjective priorities. As Kirzner has elaborated, a successful entrepreneur has an ineffable ability to notice unexploited opportunities to earn profits by addressing the hitherto overlooked or underappreciated demand of consumers.[10] If the entrepreneur is correct in his guess that resources are being underutilized or misallocated (according to consumer preferences), his reward is pure entrepreneurial profit, that is, the money left over when all the costs of an enterprise are paid, including the entrepreneur's own wages and interest on capital.

The lure of entrepreneurial profit has proved to be the most powerful incentive to uncover and satisfy heretofore unattended demand, which even consumers themselves may be unaware of in the present. We all can be said to "want" goods and services that today we can't even imagine, in the sense that once they are made available we will rush to buy them. Before there was an internet, few people consciously pined for its existence. Yet once they became aware of it, they found countless uses for its services—services that today they would have difficulty living without. What will we say that about a year from now? We can't know. One great advantage of the market order is that it encourages people to specialize in discovering such things. Since there is no limit to what entrepreneurial activity will make possible, the world is indeed open-ended.[11]

For this reason, F. A. Hayek titled an important essay "Competition as a Discovery Procedure." As Hayek writes in that essay, "competition is valuable *only* because, and so far as, its results are unpredictable and on the whole different from those which anyone has, or could have, deliberately aimed at."[12]

In a genuine market economy, entrepreneurship exists in an environment of fully free competition. Entrepreneurs with different guesses about the future state of consumer demand test their visions by carrying out their plans and submitting them to the toughest judges: consumers, who have the freedom to turn thumbs up or down on any offering. Through this process buyers and sellers learn things they would not have learned otherwise. No one can predict who will produce the next smash hit with consumers. No one can predict the next idea to take off, earning a fortune for its progenitor. Only the market will reveal it. But "the market" is not a process of disembodied forces. It is individual entrepreneurs, input owners, workers, and consumers who freely exercise their judgment about what is worthwhile and, through the price system, bring their plans into coordination.[13]

The outcome of this grappling with an uncertain future has been called spontaneous, or undesigned, order, and it is at the core of the classical-liberal, or libertarian, social vision. No successful society or economy could be consciously planned, since the requisite information for such planning is unavailable to the would-be planner. Rather, it is scattered among countless participants—incomplete, contradictory, and even unarticulated. This is Hayek's "division of knowledge."[14] The once-fashionable view that supercomputers would one day solve the "socialist calculation problem" is all but dead because Ludwig von Mises and Hayek showed that without a market economy, private property, and free exchange, prices—which are indispensable to economic calculation—would not exist and the division of knowledge could not be bridged.[15]

The critical point about entrepreneurship and spontaneous order is that it enables us to learn important things we could not otherwise learn. The market process *creates*—rather than simply reveals—what we need to know if our wants are to be satisfied. Thus all schemes to duplicate the outcomes of the market order by nonmarket methods must miss the mark. As the public choice theorist James Buchanan has elaborated this point, "the 'order' of the market emerges *only* from the *process* of voluntary exchange among the participating individuals. The 'order' is, itself, defined as the outcome of the *process* that generates it. The 'it,' the allocation–distribution result, does not, and cannot, exist independently of the trading process. Absent this process, there is and can be no 'order.' "[16]

Buchanan takes even free-market economists to task for likening market outcomes to what an omniscient being would establish on the basis of his perfect knowledge about resource supplies and consumer "utility functions." In this erroneous view, Buchanan says, the market aims at an outcome *external* to the market process and thus betrays a fundamental misunderstanding of what markets do. He writes, "The potential [market] participants *do not know until they enter the process* what their own choices will be. From this it follows that it is *logically impossible* for an omniscient designer to know, unless, of course, we are to preclude individual freedom of will."[17]

The upshot is that fully free markets are indispensable for human well-being.

Education and Entrepreneurship

The application of these insights to education should be apparent. In a free society, education is a combination of goods and services proffered by entrepreneurs to satisfy a kind of consumer demand, namely, the demand of parents to encourage the intellectual and moral development of their children so that they might make a satisfying place for themselves in the world. In economic terms, the demand for education is like any other, and its provision is not intrinsically different from the provision of other goods and services. Thus the market's exclusive role in satisfying people's unlimited and often hitherto unrecognized wants is as critical to education as to anything else.

Joseph Priestley (1733–1804), the English classical-liberal political philosopher, scientist, and religious Dissenter, understood this point. In *An Essay on the First Principles of Government, and on the Nature of Political, Civil, and Religious Liberty,* Priestley set out a Kirznerian case for a free and spontaneous market in education that few have equaled since. For Priestley, education must be left to free individuals precisely because no one can know in advance, and once and for all, what methods are best.

His writing on education emphasized the trial-and-error nature of discovery, the need for freedom, experimentation, and even "caprice," without which the "arts" cannot improve:

> [O]f all arts [including education], those stand the fairest chance of being brought to perfection, in which there is opportunity of making the most *experiments and trials* [emphasis added], and in which there are the greatest number and variety of persons employed in making them...[T]hat to establish the methods and processes of any art, before it have arrived to a state of perfection (of which no man can be a judge) is to fix it in its infancy, to perpetuate every thing that is inconvenient and awkward in it, and to cut off its future growth and improvement.[18]

Priestley is earnest in his conviction that bureaucrats can't help but stifle the stumbling, groping experimental process that is indispensable to making valuable discoveries in educational techniques. Indeed, even seemingly benign attempts by government to exclude unorthodox and eccentric ideas would damage the discovery process. We simply cannot know in advance what will work. "I may add, in this place," Priestley wrote, "that, if we argue from the analogy of education to other arts which are most similar to it, we can never expect to see human nature, about which it is employed, brought to perfection, but in consequence of *indulging unbounded liberty, and even caprice* in conducting it" (emphasis added).

Stifling the spontaneous development of education would also tend to stifle individual diversity and impose conformity, as thinkers such as Mill, Mencken, and Murray Rothbard noted. Priestly also made this point: "Instead, then, of endeavouring, by uniform and fixed systems of education, to keep mankind always the same, let us give *free scope to every thing which may bid fair for introducing more variety among us*" (emphasis added).

School Choice and the Discovery Procedure

The foregoing offers important guidance for sizing up the array of reforms known as "school choice." Specifically, it enables us to decide whether "school choice" counts as a free-market reform. We will confine our analysis to the voucher program, although it would also apply to tuition tax credits and even more so to charter-school plans.

A voucher plan would permit parents to divert some or all the money the state is prepared to allocate to their child's "public" (i.e., government-operated) school to alternative schools, private or "public." The objective is to introduce competition to education and improve all schools. As Milton Friedman, author of the voucher idea in its modern form, put in *Capitalism and Freedom*:

> Governments have, in the main, financed schooling by paying directly the costs of running educational institutions. Thus this step seemed required by the decision to subsidize schooling. Yet the two steps could readily be separated. Governments could require a minimum level of schooling financed by giving parents vouchers redeemable for a specified maximum sum per child per year if spent on "approved" educational services. Parents would then be free to spend this sum and any additional sum they themselves provided on purchasing educational services from an "approved" institution of their own choice...If present public expenditures on schooling were made available to parents regardless of where they send their children, a wide variety of schools would spring up to meet their demand.... Here, as in other fields, competitive enterprise is likely to be far more efficient in meeting consumer demand than either nationalized enterprises or enterprises run to serve other purposes.[19]

And as Milton and Rose Friedman reiterated 25 years later: "The voucher plan embodies exactly the same principle as the GI bills that provided for education benefits to military veterans. The veteran gets a voucher good only for educational expense and he is completely free to choose the school at which he uses it, provided that it satisfies certain standards."[20]

Given the intention of voucher plans to expand choice and stimulate competition, they would seem to hold promise for widening the scope of entrepreneurship in education. But appearances may be misleading. It is more likely that, despite good intentions, widespread application of the voucher principle would have the reverse effect. The Law of Unintended Consequences strikes again.

How can this be? The answer is that since the voucher will be provided by some level of government, the funds they represent would be regarded as "public money." This in turn would lead to demands that all recipient schools satisfy government requirements to prevent "the public's money" from going to unaccountable and perhaps dubious institutions. Hence, vouchers would increase government control of private schools. To the extent that schools are accountable to a government bureaucracy rather than to parents, no true free market in education can be said to exist.

Free-market voucher advocates would of course oppose new regulations on the grounds that it is parents, not the government, who are spending "their own" money. But even if the value of the voucher represented only what parents pay in school taxes, that would not change the perception that it is "public money" which must not be given out willy-nilly. Thus parents will be restricted in how they may use their vouchers. This is not hard to foresee. Today the state establishes criteria for compliance with its compulsory-attendance decree. Why would it not establish criteria for the sorts of institutions at which parents may redeem their vouchers?

Moreover, since the value of the voucher would not be adjusted according to parents' tax bills (cross-subsidies are inevitable) and since nonparents pay school taxes too, the argument for restrictions in the name of accountability would be plausible to most people.

Thus we can anticipate that any voucher program would reinforce the regulation of private schools. It is true that private schools are already regulated. But the appearance of public money going to those schools, even if it passes through parents' hands first, would bolster the case for even more regulation and standards.

Friedman's own defense of vouchers supports this expectation. He envisions vouchers being good only for "approved" schools meeting at least minimum standards. Approved by whom? Government.

But if parents may redeem their vouchers only at schools that satisfy standards set by a government entity, then they are not "completely free" with respect to their children's education.

In light of what was said earlier, government standards are inconsistent with a fully competitive entrepreneurial environment. Priestley's "trials and experimentation" and "unbounded liberty and even caprice" cannot coexist with a standard-setting bureaucracy. Where would the bureaucrats or elected officials derive the standards to impose on private schools? Would they be the result of lobbying by the educational establishment and teachers' unions, whose vested interests may be inconsistent with the educational welfare of children? Would standard setting undermine the flexibility and individualized approach to education that young human beings require? We have every reason to believe the answers would be yes. For one thing, most people who are drawn to government "service" tend to believe government should do more not less. They will find ready support in the "private" sector from rent-seekers—those who would seek profits through the political system by lobbying for favors from legislatures and school boards. We may find an analogue in the imposition of mandates on medical-insurance policies, the result of vendor-lobbyists who convince state legislators that their particular products or services are so important that every insured person should be compelled to have coverage for them.

This is not to impugn the motives of school boards and elected officials who would govern any voucher plan. This critique obtains even if they may have the best of intentions. They may sincerely reject the charge that they claim a monopoly on wisdom when it comes to educational reform and insist they are willing to listen to new and even radical ideas about schooling. The fallacy in the claim, however, is that no matter how willing they are to entertain proposals from outside the educational establishment, *they* exercise the authority to judge those proposals as either acceptable or unacceptable for the system they run. Thus in practice they implicitly claim a monopoly on wisdom.

Contrast this with the entrepreneurial environment described above. In those circumstances, educational entrepreneurs would be free to offer *any* services directly to parents. No bureaucratic filter would stand between profferer and prospective buyer. Schools would be accountable to parents and not to government officials. Parents would select schools through a variety of means: word-of-mouth referrals, consumer guides, online communities, and more. Through their children, parents would receive swift feedback about the performance of schools and novel approaches, and would be free to change schools when they were dissatisfied.

Voucher advocates who support the free market would of course oppose what they see as "excessive" regulation of private schools. But the dynamics of legislative politics offers cold comfort in the matter. Imagine that a voucher bill was introduced in a state legislature and that it contained no regulation of private schools. Any self-described school would be qualified to accept vouchers from willing parents. How long would the bill remain in that condition? We know the answer. As the legislative machinery, aided by special-interest lobbyists, began to generate qualifications for voucher eligibility, the pristine bill's advocates might object. But to what effect?

Voucher advocates seem resigned to this fact, since bills and ballot questions routinely contain qualifications for school eligibility. For example, the bill passed by the Utah legislature, and later overwhelmingly rejected by the voters, required private schools wishing to accept vouchers to "give a formal national test every year" to each student and to publish the results. A "national test" means only one thing: a standardized test approved by the education establishment. This might sound harmless, but it's actually insidious. The amount of interference implied by that condition cannot be exaggerated, since he or she who dictates the test largely dictates the curriculum. The school would have to teach to the test.[21]

Yet most voucher advocates rightly believe that without such conditions, no program stands a chance of passage. Political reality is not likely to change any time soon. Would any bill that could pass legislative or public muster be worth the effort?

The Utah case is only the latest example. The brief history of vouchers is a history of meddling with private schools, both in the United States and abroad. One of the first modern voucher programs in the United States is the Milwaukee Parental Choice Program (MPCP), a plan to permit a limited number of low-income parents to send their children to private schools. To say that the voucher schools had to comply with a list of state regulations would be an understatement. As the Wisconsin Supreme Court noted, when ruling on a First Amendment challenge to the amended MPCP in 1998,

> The legislature...placed a variety of qualification and reporting requirements on private schools choosing to participate in the original MPCP. To be eligible to participate in the original MPCP, a private school had to comply with the anti-discrimination provisions imposed

by 42 U.S.C. § 2000d and all health and safety laws or codes that apply to Wisconsin public schools.... The school additionally had to meet on an annual basis defined performance criteria and had to submit to the State certain financial and performance audits.[22]

These requirements may seem innocuous, but they can raise the cost of operation and act as barriers to entry into the market. Government bureaucracies have no particular expertise in prescribing health and safety regulations, and in fact are notorious for being subject to special-interest pressures. Efficient and innovative methods to ensure health and safety can be stymied by a slow-moving bureaucracy that wishes not to alienate politically connected providers of older, less-efficient technologies. Similarly, "defined performance criteria" may not be the criteria parents would choose in judging schools. In other words, under the MPCP, voucher schools are ultimately accountable to a government authority, not to parents in a free market.

In 1995 the state legislature amended the MPCP to include, among other things, religious schools. While the amended program removed oversight powers earlier delegated to the state superintendent of public instruction, it also mandated that "participating private schools must select on a random basis the students attending their schools under the amended program, except that they may give preference to siblings already accepted in the school. In addition, under the new 'opt-out' provision, the *private schools cannot require the students participating in the program to participate in any religious activity provided at that school*."[23]

Thus a religious school that integrates religious teachings throughout its curriculum would be ineligible for participation because opting out of religious activity would be impractical, if not impossible. Moreover, the random-selection requirement might not suit a given school. Under these new criteria, private schools would either have to conform to political considerations regardless of any inconsistency with their missions or have to disqualify themselves from the program, thereby limiting their potential customer base.

In the United States, the connection between government money and regulation is present even in higher education, as evidenced by the cases of Grove City and Hillsdale colleges. The schools refused to comply with federal civil-rights-reporting requirements on grounds they received no direct funding from the government and thus should be exempt from compliance. In *Grove City College v. Bell* (1984), the U.S. Supreme Court ruled that for the purposes of compelling compliance, it is enough that students with federal loans or grants attended the schools. Direct appropriations were not necessary for the imposition to be permitted.[24]

After surveying the experience with vouchers around the world, Herbert Walberg concluded, "Voucher programs in the United States may be too small to provide definitive evidence that universal vouchers would produce the positive outcomes predicted by advocates, but large-scale foreign voucher programs demonstrate considerable success despite *the extensive government regulation to which they are subjected*" (emphasis added).[25] Walberg delivers a similar verdict on charter-school programs: "Charter schools may have greater independence from state and local regulations than traditional schools, but they are still limited and heavily regulated in most jurisdictions in which they are allowed."[26]

Likewise, Norman LaRocque found that among European countries, "higher [government] funding of private schools tends to be associated with increased regulation of private schools."[27]

Charles Glenn studied several European countries' educational systems and warned:

> For those who believe strongly in religious schooling and fear that government influence will come with public funding, reason exists for their concern. Catholic or Protestant schools in each of the nations studied have increasingly been assimilated to the assumptions and guiding values of public schooling. This process does not [even] seem to be the result of deliberate efforts...but rather of the difficulty, for a private school playing by public rules, to maintain its distance from the common assumptions and habits of the predominant system.[28]

Similarly, Estelle James of the World Bank has reported:

> Substantial regulations usually accompany large subsidies. These regulations are similar to those applied to public schools; typically they specify hiring and firing procedures, credentials and salaries of teachers, criteria for selecting students, price and expenditures per student, and participants in the school's decision-making structure. In particular, they raise salaries and other costs while lowering private price and contributions.... Large private sectors in developed countries

are heavily subsidized, heavily controlled and, in fact, these forces lead them to behave very much like the public sector.[29]

The necessary political connection between finance and regulation has been well understood by some champions of activist government and its indispensable component, government-controlled schooling. In Europe, social democrats have long supported subsidies to private schools in order to justify "public" control of independent schools. The Fabian socialists in England did the same. In the United States, public-school advocates have firmly opposed "school choice," but some cracks in the opposition have appeared. The editors of *The New Democrat*, published by the centrist Democratic Leadership Council, have called on defenders of public schools to reconsider their staunch opposition to vouchers. They warned that the growing interest in vouchers and the establishment of private scholarship funds

> should be a wake-up call to liberal Democrats who have blocked, watered down, or gummed up reforms such as charter schools and other types of public school choice, higher standards and an end to social promotion for students, and accountability for teachers and administrators. The guardians of the educational status quo have won a few battles but are in danger of losing the war. America's great tradition of universal public education is hanging in the balance.
>
> New Democrats should continue fighting to make all public schools high-performance institutions, especially the citadels of failure and despair masquerading as schools in many inner cities. Here's a specific suggestion: When someone introduces voucher legislation in your state legislature or city council, urge your representatives to offer an amendment that would require participating private schools to (1) open their doors to all children in the community and (2) meet or exceed specified performance benchmarks to continue receiving tax-payer funds. (Indeed, that latter provision should apply to all state-supported schools, public and private.) *Such an amendment would effectively turn voucher-supported private schools into public charter schools.*
>
> "Access and accountability" amendments to voucher bills would make the following points crystal clear to school operators: If you want taxpayers' money, then you can't pick and choose from among taxpayers' children and you have to guarantee taxpayers a solid return on their investment. This will make perfect sense to most voters and even to some voucher proponents. After all, parents and taxpayers would be livid if they discovered that their local government bought a computer

system or hired someone to fix leaky roofs without a contract that spelled out what the recipient of the public money was supposed to do. But that's exactly what most voucher plans are—no-strings-attached contracts with government vendors for the provision of a vital public service.[30]

The editors have noticed something that school-choice advocates strangely overlook: "A public school is not defined by who 'owns' it, but rather by two features: universal access and accountability to the public for results." No wonder they "don't care whether public schools are run by a local school board, a group of parents, a teachers union, a Fortune 500 company, or the Little Sisters of the Poor."

Indeed. And the way to impose "universal access" and "accountability to the public for results" on private schools is for the government to give them "public money."

The leader of the Swedish Teachers' Union also recognizes this fact. Regarding Sweden's school-choice program, which has caught the interest of American voucher advocates, Eva-Lis Preisz said, "There was a lot of skepticism toward this in the beginning, but we don't have an opinion about which owner [of schools] is better... [I]t's all financed by taxes."[31]

A former undersecretary of education also acknowledged the potential for control through "school choice" in the *Politics of Education Association Yearbook*, 1990: "[We suggest a strategy to] help control many of the negative aspects, and even enhance the positive aspects of a full choice model. The state curriculum frameworks would establish a protective structure that would help ensure that all schools were attempting to provide a challenging and progressive curriculum."[32]

In his favorable review of voucher programs, Norman LaRocque argues, "Although the concern that government assistance leads to government regulation and control is real, it need not be that way. Funding and regulation are two separate policy instruments, and there is no reason why a well-designed funding policy that funds students in public and private schools in a neutral fashion must necessarily be accompanied by bad regulation."[33]

These two policy instruments may—perhaps—be separable conceptually, but they are not likely to be such in a world inhabited by politicians and rent-seeking lobbyists. As Dwight Lee points out, "As long as education is funded publicly, decisions on educational policy will be made politically. As long as decisions on educational policy are made politically, the interests of consumers will remain diffused and unorganized, and dominated by the focused and organized interests of the public school professionals."[34]

Even in the event that a voucher plan were passed with minimal regulations (although any amount would be too many), it would not be likely to stay that way. As the public schools lost students to the private schools, the public-school establishment could be counted on to react by lobbying for new rules to make the private schools less competitive. Vouchers would facilitate that effort.

One searches in vain for a pro-voucher strategy with a reasonable chance of nullifying this malignant political dynamic.[35]

Conclusion

The free-market advocates of "school choice" have the best intentions when they say vouchers (and tuition tax credits) would be a step toward educational freedom. Unfortunately, the reality of the political process makes this claim less than persuasive. Since any choice plan would contain requirements and regulations for private schools, it would necessarily forbid full blossoming of the entrepreneurial environment that is indispensable for optimal education. No government program is a suitable replacement for freedom and free market.

Many advocates of "school choice" might agree with that last statement and yet ask, "What can we do in the short run? Are we to do nothing?" This is curious. When politicians insist that some real or imagined crisis compels them to "do something (anything)," judicious people are properly skeptical and the principle *primum non nocere*—first, do no harm—comes to mind. If the likely consequences of vouchers and tax credits are what I have suggested, it would be better if those "solutions" were discarded in order to avoid making things worse. But, contrary to what "school choice" advocates think, this does not amount to doing nothing. How unfortunate that so many believe that if the government doesn't act, no one else will either!

We must avoid static analysis; any scenario must contain the elements of time and the human propensity to learn when acting to achieve ends. When left to their own devices, even people with meager resources undertake strategies to improve their situation and do so in perhaps surprisingly effective ways. This is well documented in the research James Tooley and Pauline Dixon have conducted in Africa and Asia, where people far poorer than anyone in America manage to get their children educated in private for-profit schools.[36]

To be sure, private schools in America can be expensive (though they cost less per student than the average public school). But that in itself has roots in government policy, which inflates costs artificially in a variety of ways—for example, through zoning and building codes. Moreover, in a freed education market, where "free" tax-funded government schools didn't win "customers" through predatory pricing (zero tuition), the market for private schooling would be much larger than it is today, attracting more entrepreneurs to the provision of that service. This would set off a race to find innovative and economical ways to deliver high-quality education to people of all income levels. One check on high prices would be extended or community homeschooling, in which multiple families would pool resources to jointly educate their children without running afoul of rules governing private schools. (This is not possible in all states today.) Private philanthropies would assist those who truly cannot afford education for their children, as philanthropies have always done in America.

The fact is we don't know what sorts of solutions people will discover when they realize they must do things for themselves rather than wait for politicians to ride to the rescue. The temptation to come up with a grand plan must be resisted, since no plan could account for the complexities of and variations in local situations, and no planner could know what she would need to know to plan intelligently. The relevant knowledge, which is more in the nature of "knowing how" than of "knowing that," is scattered, incomplete, and unarticulated among millions of people. No board of reformers could hope to become acquainted with that knowledge, yet decentralized, voluntary social processes (for-profit and nonprofit) make use of it every day in the solution of daunting problems—when unimpeded by the heavy hand of government. The risk of making things far worse is real and great. What Thomas Szasz calls ad hoc compassion shouldn't be allowed to override our good sense.

Primum non nocere! Laissez faire!

Notes

1. Joseph Priestley, *An Essay on the First Principles of Government, and on the Nature of Political, Civil, and Religious Liberty* (1768), Section IV, "In what manner an authoritative code of education would affect political and civil liberty" (http://tinyurl.com/5jxvn4).

2. The author dedicates this chapter to the memory of Marshall Fritz, the most articulate and passionate champion of the separation of school and state.

3. Israel M. Kirzner, *The Meaning of the Market Process: Essays in the Development of Modern Austrian Economics* (London: Routledge, 1992), 189.

4. Israel M. Kirzner, "The Perils of Regulation: A Market-Process Approach," in *Austrian Economics: A Reader*, Richard M. Ebeling, ed. (Hillsdale, MI: Hillsdale College Press, 1991), 641–44.

5. Rightly conceived, the desired constellation of educational institutions should not be regarded as a *system* because that term connotes an arrangement enclosed within boundaries set by an external authority. "Environment" is a better descriptor because it implies open-endedness. Today education suffers precisely because it is seen as a system, the boundaries of which are consciously determined by government. This chapter will argue that the reforms carrying the brand name "school choice," while perhaps expanding the boundaries to varying degrees, do not dispense with boundaries altogether and thus do not deliver on the promise of a fully competitive education market.

6. See Sheldon Richman, *Separating School and State: How to Liberate America's Families* (Fairfax, VA,: Future of Freedom Foundation, 1994).

7. Quoted in Sheldon Richman, "Individuality, Education, and Entrepreneurship," in Tibor Machan, ed., *Education in a Free Society* (Stanford, CA: Hoover Institution Press, 2000), 124.

8. The work of biochemist Roger J. Williams is illuminating in this regard. See *You Are Extraordinary* (New York: Random House, 1967); *Free and Unequal: The Biological Basis of Individual Liberty* (Indianapolis, IN: Liberty Press [1953] 1979); and "Individuality and Its Significance in Human Life," in Felix Morley, ed., *Essays in Individuality* (Philadelphia, PA: University of Pennsylvania Press, 1958).

9. See Richman, "Individuality, Education, and Entrepreneurship," 112–28.

10. Israel M. Kirzner, *Competition and Entrepreneurship* (Chicago, IL: University of Chicago Press, 1973).

11. Israel M. Kirzner, "Foreword: Advertising in an Open-Ended Universe," in Robert B. Ekelund, Jr., and David S. Saurman, *Advertising and the Market Process: A Modern Economic View* (San Francisco, CA: Pacific Research Institute, 1988), xvii.

12. F.A. Hayek, "Competition as a Discovery Procedure," in Hayek, *New Studies in Philosophy, Politics, Economics and the History of Ideas* (Chicago, IL: University of Chicago Press, 1978), 180.

13. Israel Kirzner, "Competition, Welfare, and Coordination," in Kirzner, *Competition and Entrepreneurship*, 212–42.

14. F.A. Hayek, "The Use of Knowledge in Society" (1945), in *Individualism and Economic Order* (Chicago, IL: Regnery Gateway, 1948), 77–91.

15. Israel M. Kirzner, "The Economic Calculation Debate: Lessons for Austrians," in *The Meaning of the Market Process*, 100–18.

16. James M. Buchanan, "A Note Stimulated by Reading Norman Barry, 'The Tradition of Spontaneous Order,'" *Literature of Liberty*, V (Summer 1982), 7–58, available at the Liberty Fund website (http://tinyurl .com/6lxms5).

17. Ibid.

18. Joseph Priestley, *An Essay on the First Principles of Government, and on the Nature of Political, Civil, and Religious Liberty* (1768), Section IV, "In what manner an authoritative code of education would affect political and civil liberty" (http://tinyurl.com/5jxvn4).

19. Milton Friedman, *Capitalism and Freedom*, chapter VI, "The Role of Government in Education" (Chicago, IL: University of Chicago Press, 1962), 89, 91.

20. Milton and Rose Friedman, *Free to Choose: A Personal Statement* (New York: Harcourt Brace Jovanovich, 1980), 161.

21. See Sheldon Richman, "Ersatz School Choice," Foundation for Economic Education, November 9, 2007, (http://tinyurl.com/yhbvvoo).

22. *Jackson v. Benson*, Wisconsin Supreme Court, June 10, 1998 (http://tinyurl .com/6378qo).

23. Ibid.

24. Jacob Huebert, "Independent Schools at Risk," *The Freeman*, September 1999, (http://tinyurl.com/nxnyo4).

25. Herbert J. Walberg, *School Choice: The Findings* (Washington, DC: Cato Institute, 2007), 55.

26. Ibid., 31.

27. Norman LaRocque, "Lessons from New Zealand," in David Salisbury and James Tooley, eds., *What Americans Can Learn from School Choice in Other Countries* (Washington, DC: Cato Institute, 2005), 127, 128.

28. Charles L. Glenn, *Choice in Schools in Six Nations* (Washington: U.S. Department of Education, 1989), 210–11; quoted in Joseph L. Bast, David Hammer, and Douglas Dewey, "Vouchers and Educational Freedom: A Debate," Cato Institute Policy Analysis No. 269, March 12, 1997, 37.

29. Estelle James, "The Public–Private Division of Responsibility for Education," in *International Encyclopedia of Education*, 2d ed. (Oxford: Elsevier Science, 1994), 782, quoted in Bast et al., 38.

30. "Counterpunching on School Vouchers" (editorial), *The New Democrat*, May 1, 1999 (http://tinyurl.com/2cwlqc).

31. Malin Rising, "School Choice in Sweden Attracts Interest Abroad," *Arkansas Democrat Gazette* (AP), July 27, 2008, 12A.

32. Quoted in Marshall Fritz, "Can You Say En-ti-tle-ment?" *The Education Liberator*, vol. 2, no. 6, July 1996, Alliance for the Separation of School and State (http://tinyurl.com/685fzv).

33. LaRocque, 127.

34. Dwight R. Lee, "The Political Economy of Educational Vouchers," *The Freeman*, July 1986, (http://tinyurl.com/bmujao).

35. Robert Enlow found a range of regulatory regimes when he surveyed the 21 U.S. school-choice programs. Conceding a degree of subjective judgment, Enlow concluded that "for reasons that have nothing to do with improving education for children, [unreasonable] restrictions...do exist among school choice programs. A few control classroom content. Others exert control over the schools' admission policies, hindering their ability to select the students that best match the strengths of their program and staff. Still others require schools to implement testing regimes that might embody goals and priorities different from those of students." Robert C. Enlow, *Grading School Choice: Evaluating School Choice Programs by the Friedman Gold Standard*, The Friedman Foundation for Educational Choice, February 2008, 20–21.

36. James Tooley and Pauline Dixon, *"Private Education Is Good for the Poor: A Study of Private Schools Serving the Poor in Low-Income Countries,"* Cato Institute White Paper, December 7, 2005 (http://tinyurl.com /ygyjfx).

Chapter 6

Revolution at the Grassroots in Developing Countries: Implications for School Choice in America

Pauline Dixon and James Tooley

Introduction and Two Propositions

For the last decade, we have been working in developing countries—especially in sub-Saharan Africa and India—cataloguing and, more recently, assisting in the development of the extraordinary educational revolution that is taking place. For anyone interested in how the poor are learning to help themselves, it is a wonderfully uplifting story.[1] It's a story of how, in slums and shantytowns around the developing world, the vast majority of poor school children are attending low-cost private schools, affordable even to parents on minimum wages. It's a story of how entrepreneurs have set up these schools, often against great odds, and how untrained teachers within them are able to bring out more from their children than those in public schools. And it's a story, above all, of how parents find that the low-cost private schools are accountable to them—in stark contrast to the public schools, where parents see teachers able to get away with little or no teaching.

The evidence we've accumulated over the years suggests two propositions that we believe any school choice program would need to meet—at least if it is to start bringing in any of the virtues of the private education market that we see in developing countries. It is likely that these are minimum requirements, rather than all that is required—we leave this question hanging, pending further evidence and exploration. These two propositions are:

1. Freedom: Give freedom to educational entrepreneurs to open places for learning, and to innovate within them. A system that has high barriers to entry and restrictive regulations, and that does not capitalize on the potential of entrepreneurs willing to enter the educational space, is unlikely to exhibit the advantages that a market in education can bring.
2. Price: Ensure that parents have a monetary interest in their schools—or, in plain language, parents must pay fees; whether this is the entire value or some proportion we leave to further discussion. Without this monetary contribution, parents are unlikely to bring to bear the required pressure on their schools to keep standards high and to keep entrepreneurs innovating. In particular, do not assume that even poor parents will be unwilling to pay some or all of their fees. Furthermore, don't assume that poor parents will not *prefer* to pay school fees if this means their schools are accountable to them.

An important question is whether this evidence and experience can offer much by way of hope for, or example to, the school choice movement in America. It seems to us that there is some "good news" and "bad news" in this regard. We'll come to these in the final section. But first, what is happening in developing countries?

The Grassroots Revolution

A grassroots educational revolution is taking place in developing countries. Responsibilities for education are being transferred de facto to the private sector (providing parents, in other words, with "choice"), through the rapid growth of private schools, rather than de jure (for instance, through the kinds of school choice reforms contemplated in America). In Haiti, for example, privatization is reported to have occurred "by default, one could almost say by despair, rather than by deliberate intention of the State,"[2] and the situation in Uganda, Tanzania, and Malawi is described in almost the same way where "in many cases the expanded role of the non-state sector has in many cases been by default (or despair) rather than by design."[3] The fact that private schools for the poor have "mushroomed" in developing countries is widely documented. For example, evidence from India (Haryana, Uttar Pradesh, Rajasthan, and Calcutta), Pakistan (Lahore), and Uganda, Malawi, and Nigeria reveal that private schools serving the poor have expanded rapidly.[4]

The reasons often stated for this expansion are the poor quality and insufficient quantity of government schools. *The Human Development Report* notes that in India and Pakistan "poor households cited teacher absenteeism in public schools as their main reason for choosing private ones"[5] and *The World Development Report* notes that "many governments are falling short on their obligations, especially to poor people," in not providing sufficient school places.[6]

However, although it is generally recognized that private schools for the poor exist and are growing in number, many critics regard them as being of poor quality, as promoting inequality and encouraging the demise of the government system. So what is required, these commentators say, is more and better public education. According to the World Bank, "There is no silver bullet...Even if we know what is to be done, it may be difficult to get it done. Despite the urgent needs of the world's poor people, and the many ways services have failed them, quick results will be hard to come by. Many of the changes involve fundamental shifts in power—something that cannot happen overnight. Making services work for poor people requires patience."[7] Kevin Watkins, formally of Oxfam and now at the United Nations Development Programme (UNDP) wrote, "parents should not withdraw their children from the public education system and put them in private schools," for this "reduces parental pressure to improve government schools."[8]

But parents don't seem to see it that way. Findings from the research we carried out between 2003 and 2006, funded by the John Templeton Foundation, and more recently by Orient Global, show that poor people appear not to be listening to the World Bank or the UNDP. They haven't got time to be "patient," for it's their children's lives at stake.

Our research set out to discover how many private unaided schools existed in low-income areas—slums and shantytowns, poor villages in areas near to major cities—and to determine their nature and extent and in particular how they compared in quality with the government alternative. Part of the research conducted censuses of low-income areas in India, Ghana, Nigeria, and Kenya. Research teams combed poor areas, walking down every alleyway and every lane looking for schools. They asked street traders and taxi drivers where the poor sent their children to school.

India, Ghana, and Nigeria

The research in India, Ghana, and Nigeria revealed a similar picture for urban and peri-urban areas: the large majority of schools in the low-income areas investigated are unaided private schools, either recognized/registered or unrecognized/unregistered in status (table 6.1). In three low-income zones of the city of Hyderabad—Charminar, Bhadurpura, and Bandlaguda, totaling an area of 28 square kilometers—918 schools were found, out of which 60 percent were private unaided (private aided schools are very much like government schools; they are run by private management, but salaries of teachers are paid by the state). Of children in these three zones, 65 percent attend private unaided schools. The story is similar in Ghana and Nigeria. In the district of Ga, Ghana, and Lagos State, Nigeria, 75 and 66 percent of schools, respectively, are private unaided, with 64 percent of children in Ga and 75 percent of children in Lagos State attending private unaided schools. More

Table 6.1 Number and proportion of schools, by school type and pupil enrollment

	Hyderabad, India			Ga, Ghana			Lagos State, Nigeria		
	No. of schools	% schools	% pupils	No. of schools	% schools	% pupils	No. of schools	% schools	% pupils
Government	320	34.9	24.0	197	25.3	35.6	185	34.3	26.0
Private aided	49	5.3	11.4	n/a	n/a	n/a	n/a	n/a	n/a
Private (unaided) unrecognized or unregistered	335	36.5	23.1	177	22.7	15.3	233	43.1	33.0
Private (unaided) recognized or registered	214	23.3	41.5	405	52.0	49.1	122	22.6	42.0
Total	918	100	100	779	100	100	540	100	100

parents are choosing to pay to send their children to private schools than choose the "free" government alternative.

The majority of these private schools are run as businesses by entrepreneurs who live in the communities themselves, who have been alerted to the educational needs of children in their area. Having analyzed thousands of schools' income and expenditure schedules, we see that private schools, in general, can be profitable institutions. Schools charge fees, which make up the vast majority of their income. For instance, in the Hyderabad study, mean monthly fees at fourth grade were Rs.78.17 ($1.74) in unrecognized and Rs.102.55 ($2.28) in recognized private schools in the slums— about 4.2 and 5.5 percent respectively of the monthly wage for a breadwinner on a typical minimum wage of about Rs.78 per day. However, not all children pay fees, as free and concessionary places are generally provided for orphans and children from large families.[9] Reasons for this philanthropy range from a genuine concern for those who are precluded from private schooling because of their financial circumstances to a need by the school owner to be seen by the community to be running a caring institution. Obviously, if the private schools weren't making a surplus, then money would not be ploughed into this philanthropic endeavor.

Teachers in private schools generally live in the community itself and are paid well below the rate of government school teachers, yet their commitment to teaching and to the children is much higher than the government teachers who are often bussed into a shantytown or slum because they have been seconded there by government officials. They know little of the communities or the children. In private schools there is a greater amount of teaching activity going on than in government schools in all the countries visited. For example, when researchers called unannounced on a class in private schools in Hyderabad, India, teaching was going on in 97.5 percent of private recognized schools, and in 90.5 percent of private unrecognized schools, compared with 74.6 percent in government schools (see table 6.2). So, even in the case of private schools that are unregistered, teachers are carrying out their duties more than those in government schools.

Private schools were also found, in general, to be better equipped than the government alternatives, with better facilities and inputs, such as drinking water, toilets, and lower pupil–teacher ratios.

Table 6.2   Teacher activity of grade four/five

	Activity of the teacher	Hyderabad, India	Ga, Ghana	Lagos, Nigeria
Private recognized/recognized	Teaching	97.5	75.0	87.9
	Nonteaching	2.0	19.8	11.1
	Absent	0.5	5.2	1.0
Private unrecognized/unregistered	Teaching	90.5	66.4	87.0
	Nonteaching	5.5	24.4	12.0
	Absent	4.0	9.2	1.1
Government	Teaching	74.6	56.7	67.3
	Nonteaching	19.7	28.3	24.5
	Absent	5.7	15.0	8.2

Finally, we tested around 24,000 children, taken from a stratified random sample of schools within these poor communities. Children were tested in key curriculum subjects, and questionnaires given to children, their parents, teachers, and school managers, as well as IQ tests to children and their teachers, to elicit data to control for a wide range of background variables, including peer-group variables. This research showed that private schools everywhere were outperforming the government schools in the key curriculum subjects—even after controlling for background variables. In Lagos State, for instance, the mean math score advantage over government schools was about 14 and 19 percentage points, respectively, in private registered and unregistered schools, while in English it was 22 and 29 percentage points. After controlling for background variables, and, given that students were not randomly assigned to the different school management types, the school choice process, we still found large differences, although reduced, in favor of private education. In Lagos State, Nigeria, the predicted score in mathematics was 45.1 percent for an average sample child in government school, 53.5 percent for the same average child in an unregistered private school, and 57.6 percent in a registered private school. For English the predicted score for an average sample child in government school was also 45.1 percent, while there was no significant difference between attainment in both types of private school—the predicted score for the same child was 64.4 percent.

Significantly, private schools were found to be outperforming government schools for a fraction of the teacher costs—likely to be the largest part of recurrent expenditure in schools. Even when the per-pupil teacher cost was computed (to take into account the fact that class sizes were largest in government schools), private schools came out less expensive: in the government schools in Lagos State, for instance, per-pupil teacher costs were nearly two and a half times higher in government than in private schools.[10]

Kenya

The research carried out in Nairobi, Kenya, had a slightly different focus: it set out to investigate the impact of the introduction of free primary education (FPE) in public schools, to much acclaim from international agencies, in January 2003. The research was carried out 10 months after the introduction of FPE, in and around the largest slum in East Africa, Kibera. In all, the research found 76 private schools in Kibera, enrolling 12,132 students, all of which appeared to be off any radar as far as the government and international development agencies were concerned.

Development agencies' excitement about FPE seems to arise because it was reported to have led to a massive increase in enrollment—an extra 1.3 million primary school children across Kenya, with a reported increase of over 48 percent in Nairobi alone. However, these headline figures don't take into account what was happening in the private schools in the slums—because no one seems to have either been aware of their existence or thought they were worth bothering about. What difference would it make to these headline figures if changes in enrollment in these private schools were also taken into account?

Our researchers asked managers, in both private and public schools, how FPE had affected their primary school enrollment. They also asked if managers knew of any private schools that had closed altogether because of FPE. What we found completely contradicted the accepted wisdom of the development experts.

True, FPE had dramatically increased the number of students enrolled in all five government primary schools reportedly serving Kibera and located on its outskirts. The total increase reported was 3,296 students, an increase of 57 percent on the reported earlier enrollment—an even higher figure than the reported headline increase figure—but this might have been anticipated, given that government schools on the periphery of slum areas would be expected to have taken larger increases than schools further removed. It is in any case a dramatic increase, part of the reported increase in enrollment of 1.3 million nationwide.

However, taking into account what was happening in the private schools in the slums, a totally different picture emerges. Most of the low-cost private schools had experienced a net decline in enrollment. This was not the case in all schools—around 30 percent of the schools reported that enrollment had either stayed roughly the same or declined initially but since recovered, or even had actually increased. Adding together the decline in the majority of schools, and subtracting the increase in the others, gave a *net decrease in private sector enrollment of 6,571—far greater than the growth in public school enrollment.* That is, far from leading to a massive increase in the number of children in school, as the official figures acclaimed, there seemed to have been a large decrease.

However, this was not the end of the story. We were given the names of 33 private schools that school managers told us had closed since the introduction of FPE. We went searching for the owners of these former private schools. And after much detective work, we were able to locate and interview 32 of them. We also uncovered an additional three private schools that had closed since FPE was introduced, names of which had not been given to us by existing school managers. Not all of these 35 private schools had closed because of FPE; in fact, two of the schools had relocated and were still open, while six had closed because of demolition work due to the building of a by-pass through Kibera. And two had closed, the managers candidly told us, because of mismanagement or lack of funds, unconnected with FPE. However, in the 25 schools that had closed specifically because of FPE, a total of *4,600 children* were reported to have been enrolled in the primary sections.

Pulling all this information together, we could arrive at an estimate of the net decrease in the number of students enrolled from Kibera as a result of the introduction of FPE. In private schools as a whole, it seemed that enrollment had declined by 11,171 since the introduction of FPE. Set against the increase in government schools of 3,296, this meant overall a net *decrease* of 7,875 in enrollment of primary school children since the introduction of FPE. That is, there

Table 6.3   Summary of net increase/decrease in enrollment in Kibera (2003)

Category	Increase/decrease in enrollment
Net decrease in enrollment in existing private schools	−6,571
Net decrease in enrollment in closed private schools	−4,600
Net increase in enrollment in government schools	+3,296
Total net increase/decrease in enrollment	−7,875

may have been about 8,000 *fewer* students from Kibera enrolled in primary schools than before FPE was introduced (table 6.3).

Of course, the figure could be inaccurate, as it is based on the *reported* increase and decline in school enrollment by school managers. These may be incorrect simply because the managers may have remembered incorrectly. Or they may have felt some incentive to exaggerate their decline in student numbers if they felt this would lead to financial or other assistance. It also assumes that all children who have left Kibera private primary schools could only have gone to the five primary government schools bordering Kibera, but they may have enrolled at other government schools, once those bordering Kibera reached capacity. And children may also have moved to other towns or rural areas, perhaps through natural movement of families in and out of the slum areas—but we had no way of quantifying this "natural" movement unconnected with FPE.

Whatever reasonable objections there are to the figures, they clearly pointed to the need for a more sober assessment of the net impact of FPE on enrollment. They dramatically showed that you ignore enrollment in private schools for the poor at your peril. And they demonstrated that the strategy of FPE succeeds above all in "crowding out" private schools that were already serving the poor.

At best, even if the reported figures were exaggerated by *a factor of four*, this would still mean that the net impact of FPE was *the same number of children enrolled in primary streams*—the increase in government enrollment merely reflecting a transfer from private to government schools. Far from being a huge success story for aid in Africa, the FPE that is so prominently held up as being something to be emulated by others may at best have only led to a straight transfer of children from private schools in the slums to the public schools on the periphery. Worse than that, it has destroyed a not insignificant

number of private businesses that were gainfully employing workers without the need for international aid funding—just the sort of
self-sustaining economic activity that is responsible for the rise of
nations out of poverty.

Our researchers went back to Kibera in late 2007. Things seem to
have improved greatly for the private schools since then. Now, four
years after the introduction of FPE, we found 116 private schools
operating in Kibera, an increase in the total number of schools in
the Kibera education market of 53 percent (40 schools). However,
of the 116 found in 2007, only 58 were in the original 2003 list of 76;
that is, 18 of the private schools found in 2003 had since closed. In
the 18 schools that had closed since 2003, there were a total of 1,688
pupils enrolled at the time of the earlier survey. In the 58 schools
that have remained open, enrollment had increased from 10,444
children in 2003 to 16,330 in 2007, an increase in enrollment of 56.4
percent. The newly located schools (58) had a total enrollment of
11,553. Overall, enrollment in the private sector had increased from
12,132 pupils to 27,883, an increase of 130 percent. Meanwhile,
enrollment in the government schools—where many children will
not be from the slums—was up from 9,126 to 11,214, an increase of
only 23 percent (table 6.4).

Clearly, many more parents have decided that FPE in government schools is less desirable than a place in a budget private school;
it does not matter that fees have to be paid. One indicator of quality
is clear from the study. In the 2007 study, the pupil–teacher ratio in
government schools was 88:1, up from 60:1 in the 2003 study. In the
private schools, the pupil–teacher ratio in the 2007 study was 28:1,
up from 21:1 in the 2003 study. This alone could indicate one of the
benefits parents perceive from the private schools.

Even though the World Bank gave Kenya one of its largest education grants of $55 million in order to help set up FPE, it would

Table 6.4   Kibera study, enrollment in public and private schools

	Enrollment	
Year of study	*Private*	*Government*
2003	12,132	9,126
2007	27,883	11,214
% increase	130	23

seem from these initial findings that this was money not well spent. Because parents still had a choice, they turned their backs on what government and aid agencies prescribed for them. They have chosen to go their own way, paying for education they feel is better for their children, that they are able to choose, and where the schools are accountable to them. One father, who had first moved his daughter from a low-cost private school in the slum to a government school on the outskirts but had then moved her back to the private school, summed up succinctly his own views on the relative merits of public and private schools by way of analogy. "If you go to a market," he said, "and are offered free fruit and vegetables, they will be rotten. If you want fresh fruit and veg, you have to pay for them."

Lessons for School Choice in America?

So now we return to the "good news" and the "bad news". We started with two propositions that emerged from our research and experiences of over a decade in developing countries. Without satisfying these two propositions—of *freedom* for entrepreneurs to operate and a *price* mechanism for accountability to parents—it seemed unlikely to us that a school choice program could move to anything like the benefits of real markets in education. The "good news" is this: it seems that our two propositions provide prima facie satisfying answers to two of the major objections that Milton and Rose Friedman reported were being used against the introduction of school choice programs in America:

One of these fundamental objections they characterized as "doubt about new schools."[11] Given that private schools were then either "parochial schools or elite academies," critics of the voucher proposal wanted to know what reason there was "to suppose that alternatives will really arise?" The Friedmans were convinced that "a market would develop where it does not exist today…attract[ing] many entrants, both from public schools and from other occupations." Their conviction came from talking to many people about vouchers: "We have been impressed by the number of persons who said something like, 'I have always wanted to teach [or run a school] but I couldn't stand the educational bureaucracy, red tape, and general ossification of the public schools. Under your plan, I'd like to try my hand at starting a school.'"[12]

The evidence that we've outlined from developing countries supports their confidence in the entrepreneurial spirit: in developing countries, at least, educational entrepreneurs *do* emerge to provide educational opportunities, including for some of the poorest members of society. They emerge because parents and poor communities are concerned about education; it is a fundamental priority. When they have (well-founded) doubts about the efficiency and effectiveness of public schools, they'll create alternatives of their own. Could the same be true in America? Here we may have our first bit of "bad news": the key would seem to be that barriers to entry are low in the countries we surveyed, and this is likely a major reason why entrepreneurs respond in the ways they do. In America, barriers to entry may well be rather high and may also have been difficult to bring down in reform programs—we're sympathetic to the arguments of John Merrifield in both these respects.[13]

Some might argue that barriers to entry are also rather high in some developing countries and that this isn't a major difference between the cases we've explored and America. For instance, India has a very imposing regulatory regime for the opening and subsequent government recognition of schools that seems prima facie hard to satisfy—and the situation is likely to get more difficult with the introduction of the Right to Education Act. However, as we've discussed elsewhere, such regulatory regimes are in practice usually ignored, subject to unofficial payments being made to government inspectors.[14] In America they probably won't be so easily ignored. So although the "good news" is that our evidence shows the willingness of educational entrepreneurs to enter the market, *pace* the objections to choice highlighted by Friedman, the "bad news" is that in America substantial reform will be needed to get rid of barriers to entry where they are high before these advantages can be realized. At least this provides a useful parameter by which the success of school choice reforms in America can be judged—if barriers to entry are kept too high, then they are unlikely to succeed.

Back to the "good news": Our evidence from developing countries also helps challenge the second of the fundamental objections to vouchers in America, that prosperous families would "top-up," or supplement, the government's provision with their own funds. The Friedmans call this the "economic class issue."[15] Critics argued that topping-up vouchers would penalize poor parents who wouldn't want to spend their resources on education. The Friedmans replied that "this view...seems to us another example of the tendency of intellectuals to denigrate parents who are poor. Even the very poorest can—and do—scrape up a few extra dollars to improve the quality of their children's schooling."[16] The evidence from developing countries appears to support this argument: Some of the poorest parents on this planet do appear willing to "scrimp and save" to pay for their children's education; this evidence is available to inform the parallel school choice debate within America. Some might believe there is more "bad news" here because the costs of schooling in the areas surveyed are not nearly as high as those in America, probably because of the lower barriers of entry. However, the Friedmans don't require that the poor should be able to pay "the whole of the present cost of public schooling," so it is feasible that the evidence from developing countries can support their claims.[17] The only potential "bad news" for this argument, we believe, comes from the possibility that poor parents are willing to pay because there is no tradition of a welfare state in the countries surveyed—so poor parents having nothing else to fall back on are prepared to pay for schooling to help their children escape poverty. In America, attitudes of the poor to spending their own funds for schooling may be quite different, given reliance amongst some of the poor on various forms of welfare.

So in the end, this chapter does not pretend to conclude with any political manifesto for reform. We are aware of the immense political difficulties that introducing anything like the two propositions highlighted at the beginning of this chapter would bring about. Indeed, in our recent brief survey of various school choice programs around the world, we suggested that only Sweden's "voucher" program comes remotely close to the first proposition, and the second is not met anywhere.[18]

In that survey we also recognized many of the political difficulties that arise with introducing school choice reforms, agreeing with Milton Friedman's frustrations about the possibilities of educational reform in America on many levels: First, we agreed with him on the tiny scale of experimental reforms in America. Taking all of the school choice reform programs in America together, Friedman noted, "They cover only a small fraction of all children in the country."[19] And we noted Friedman's expression of frustration over

50 years of advocating vouchers with the "adamant and effective opposition of trade union leaders and educational administrators to any change that would in any way reduce their control of the educational system."[20] For instance, he gave the example of his involvement in trying to bring about a universal voucher system rather than a small-scale experiment in the state of California in 1993 and 2000. In both cases, he wrote, "The initiatives were carefully drawn up and the voucher sums moderate." The costings had been carefully worked out to show the advantages. Public opinion polls only nine months or so before the elections showed "a sizeable majority in favor of the initiative," plus "a sizable group of fervent supporters" active. But then, on each occasion about six months before the election "opponents of vouchers launched a well-financed and thoroughly unscrupulous campaign against the initiative. Television ads blared that vouchers would break the budget," even though the carefully worked-out sums clearly showed a reduction in government spending, given that the vouchers for private schools were "only a fraction of what government was spending per student." Most sinisterly, for Friedman, "teachers were induced to send home with their students misleading propaganda against the initiative. Dirty tricks of every variety were financed from a very deep purse." In each case, these tactics won the day—"the result was to convert the initial majority into a landslide defeat." The same occurred, Friedman reported, in Washington State, Colorado, and Michigan. "Opposition like this explains why progress has been so slow in such a good cause."[21]

The reasons Friedman gave for this slow progress also seemed plausible: "centralization, bureaucratization, and unionization have enabled teachers' union leaders and educational administrators to gain effective control of government elementary and secondary schools. The union leaders and educational administrators rightly regard extended parental choice through vouchers and tax-funded scholarships as the major threat to their monopolistic control. So far, they have been extremely successful in blocking any significant change."[22]

Usefully, Friedman also outlined the various elements that any genuine school choice program might require: "Change the organization of elementary schooling and secondary schooling from top-down to bottom-up. Convert to a system in which parents choose the schools their children attend—or, more broadly, the educational services their children receive, whether in a brick-and-mortar school or on DVDs or over the Internet or whatever alternative the ingenuity of man can conceive. Parents would pay for educational services with whatever subsidy they received from the government plus whatever sum they want to add out of their own resources. Producers would be free to enter or leave the industry and would compete to attract students. As in other industries, such a competitive free market would lead to improvements in quality and reductions in cost."[23]

The key problem for Friedman was "how to get from here to there."[24] In this chapter, we've looked at the issue from the other end, as it were. We've looked at a system that in some sense *is already* "there," admittedly in countries that are much poorer than America, so where the educational standards that arise are not necessarily what might be desired in America, and where the barriers to entry (at least de facto, if not de jure) are very low. Ultimately, we may have to be very cautious in drawing lessons of our work for the school choice movement in America. We can agree with Milton Friedman that the desired changes are likely to come from the "bottom up," not the "top down"; our evidence shows places where this indeed is happening, to some great effect. Perhaps hope—"good news"—is at hand here too, though. We've suggested elsewhere that out of the genuine education markets that exist, particularly in India and China, are likely to emerge intensely competitive, brand-name "chains" of schools, competing amongst other things on price. Once these start emerging on a large enough scale, with strong enough academic and other educational results, they are likely to start entering the American market.[25] Once this happens, there could be a very strong movement for the breaking down of barriers to entry in education that will change forever the political environment that makes reform so difficult in America. These emerging chains may in the end provide the answer to Friedman's question of how we get from here to there.

Notes

1. For the complete story, see Tooley, James (2009) *The Beautiful Tree: A Personal Journey into How the World's Poorest People Are Educating Themselves*, Penguin, New Delhi, and Cato Institute, Washington DC.

2. Salmi, J. (2000) Equity and Quality in Private Education: The Haitian Paradox, *Compare*, 30(2), 163–178, (p. 165)

3. Rose, P. (2002) Is the Non-State Education Sector Serving the Needs of the Poor? Evidence from East and Southern Africa, Paper prepared for DfID Seminar in preparation for 2004 World Development Report (p. 15).

4. De, A., Majumdar, M., Samson, M., and Noronha, C. (2002) Private Schools and Universal Elementary education, in: R. Govinda (Ed.) India Education Report: A Profile of Basic Education (Oxford University Press, Oxford), pp. 131–150; Nambissan, G. B. (2003) Educational deprivation and primary school provision: a study of providers in the city of Calcutta. IDS Working Paper 187 (Brighton, Institute of Development Studies); Adelabu, M. and Rose, P. (2004) Non-State Provision of Basic Education in Nigeria, in: G. Larbi, M. Adelabu, P. Rose, D. Jawara, O. Nwaorgu, and S. Vyas (Eds.) Nigeria: Study of Non-State Providers of Basic Services, Non-State Providers of Basic Services DfID, Birmingham); Rose, P. (2002) Is the Non-State Education Sector Serving the Needs of the Poor? Evidence from East and Southern Africa, Paper prepared for DfID Seminar in preparation for 2004 World Development Report

5. UNDP (2003) Human development report 2003 (United Nations Development Programme, New York). (UNDP, 2003, p. 112).

6. World Bank (2003) Making Services Work for Poor People: World Development Report 2004 (World Bank/Oxford University Press, Washington Oxford). (p. 3).

7. Ibid. p. 18.

8. Watkins, K. (2004) Private Education and ' "Education for All" — or How Not to Construct an Evidence-Based Argument, *Economic Affairs*, 24(4), 8–11 (p. 11).

9. Tooley, J., and Dixon, P., (2005) Is There a Conflict between "Commercial Gain and Concern for the Poor"?: Evidence from Private schools for the Poor in India and Nigeria? *Economic Affairs*, IEA, London, pp. 20–26.

10. For further details on the research methods and some of these results see, for example, Tooley, J., and Dixon, P. (2005) *Private Education Is Good for the Poor—A Study of Private Schools Serving the Poor in Low-Income Countries*, CATO Institute, Washington DC; Tooley, J., and Dixon, P. (2007) Private Schooling for Low-Income Families: A Census and Comparative Survey in East Delhi, India, *International Journal of Educational Development*, 27, 2, pp. 205–219; Tooley, J., Dixon, P., and Gomathi, S. V (2007) Private Schools and the Millennium Development Goal of Universal Primary Education: A census and comparative survey in Hyderabad, India, *Oxford Review of Education*, 33, 5; Tooley, J., Dixon, P. and Olaniyan, O. (2005) Private and Public Schooling in low-income areas of Lagos State, Nigeria: A Census and Comparative Survey, *International Journal of Educational Research*, 43, pp. 125–146.

11. Friedman, M., and Friedman, R. (1980) *Free to Choose*, Harmonsworth, Pelican Books, England, p. 204.
12. Ibid, pp. 204–05.
13. See Merrifield, John (2001) *The School Choice Wars*, Lanham, Maryland, The Scarecrow Press, Inc., and Merrifield, John (2005), Choice as an Education Reform Catalyst: Lessons from Chile, Milwaukee, Florida, Cleveland, Edgewood, New Zealand, and Sweden, in: Salisbury, David and Tooley, James (Eds.) *What Americans Can Learn from School Choice in Other Countries*, Cato Institute, Washington DC, pp. 175–220.
14. See Tooley, James and Dixon, Pauline, (2005) An Inspector Calls: The Regulation of "Budget" Private Schools in Hyderabad, Andhra Pradesh, India, *International Journal of Educational Development*. 25, 269–285.
15. Friedman, M., and Friedman, R. (1980) *Free to Choose*, Harmonsworth, Pelican Books, England, p. 203.
16. Ibid, pp. 203–04.
17. Ibid, p. 204
18. See Tooley, James (2008) *E.G. West: Economic Liberalism and the Role of the State in Education*, Continuum, London and New York.
19. Friedman, Milton, (2006a), Prologue: A Personal Retrospective, in: Enlow, Robert, C., and Ealy, Lenore T. (Eds.), *Liberty and Learning: Milton Friedman's Voucher Idea at Fifty*, Cato Institute, Washington DC, p. ix.
20. Ibid.
21. Ibid, p. x.
22. Friedman, Milton, (2006b), Epilogue: School Choice Turns 50, but the Fun Is Just Beginning, in: Enlow, Robert, C., and Ealy, Lenore T. (Eds.), *Liberty and Learning: Milton Friedman's Voucher Idea at Fifty*, Cato Institute, Washington, DC, p. 157.
23. Ibid, p. 156.
24. Ibid.
25. Tooley, James, (2006), Education Reclaimed, in Booth, Philip (Ed.), *Towards a Liberal Utopia?*, Continuum International Publishing Group, London, New York, pp. 27–30.

Chapter 7

Do Children Have a "Right" to an Education?

C. Bradley Thompson

> For it is correct to take care of the young first, so that they will be the best possible, just as a good farmer properly takes care of the young plants first, and after this of the others as well.
>
> *Socrates in Plato's* Euthyphro

One of the most deeply held assumptions of the modern world is that education is a fundamental human right.[1] This "right" to an education is said to be so basic, so essential to human dignity, that only the State can assume the responsibility of providing it for every child because not every parent will ensure that his or her children will be properly educated. The classic statement upholding and extending the logic of this principle is contained in the United Nation's Universal Declaration of Human Rights, which states, "Everyone has the right to education. Education shall be free, at least in the elementary and fundamental stages. Elementary education shall be compulsory (Article 26, item 1)."[2]

In the United States, this assumption has dominated education policy for well over 100 years, and it is the moral premise underlying the Bush administration's "No Child Left Behind" Act.[3] American conservatives, no less than liberals, believe that education is a basic human right that must be provided by the government. Not surprisingly, then, even most conservative supporters of vouchers and charter schools do so on the grounds that such reforms are the best means to guarantee that all children have their right to an education fully satisfied. If there is one issue on which almost all Republicans and Democrats agree, it is this: that all children have a right to a government-sponsored education.

What could this extraordinary claim mean in theory and practice? What could it possibly mean to say everyone has the right to a free, compulsory education?

This chapter reopens the case of children's rights (and by extension the rights of parents), and, more particularly, it investigates the commonly held assumption that children have an inalienable human right to an education. Our goal is to determine whether the assumption can be validated philosophically or whether it is simply a sentimental prejudice. The claim that children have a right to an education must be examined within the broader context of children's rights per se and the relationship of those rights to those of parents. To that end, we shall, first, highlight the remarkably complicated nature of our subject by posing a number of probing questions; second, elucidate a general theory of rights that will inform our analysis; third, establish the metaphysical foundations of the rights of children and those of their parents; fourth, delineate the rights and responsibilities of parents; and fifth, define the rights and responsibilities of children. In the end, we shall argue that children do indeed have a limited rights claim to be educated in some way, but the great challenge is to define the nature and provider of that right.

Defining the Problem

Applying the concept of "rights" to children is a remarkably complicated problem that raises a host of challenging questions that go well beyond the issue of education. The fundamental questions are these: Do children have the same rights as adults, no rights at all, something in between, or something different? If children do have rights, what are they and from what source are they derived? Are they "natural" (i.e., metaphysical) or "conventional" (i.e., man-made)? Are the rights of children endowed by God, a gift of society, or grounded in some other source? When and how do children acquire the full rights afforded to adults? Do children have a right to liberty or property? Do children have positive rights-claims to be fed, clothed, sheltered, protected, and even educated? If so, from whom should that right be satisfied—their parents or the State? To what kind and to how much education are children entitled by right? Do they have a right to decide whether or not to go to school?

Inseparably linked to and significantly complicating the question of children's rights is the issue of parental rights. Again, consider some of the basic questions: What are the rights of parents and from whence are they derived? Are they "natural" or "conventional" rights? What is the relationship of parental rights to children's rights? These fundamental questions about parental rights give rise to several corollary questions: Do parents have property rights in their children? Do they have limited or unlimited rights to govern their children as they see fit? Do parents have the right to initiate force against their children, and, if so, how much? What actions by parents would constitute a violation of the rights of their children? Do parents have a right to control the education of their children, or is that a matter better left to the State?

To translate the theory of individual rights into practice, we must also consider how these rights are to be protected and by whom, which means that we must also describe the role played by government in protecting the rights of individuals. The concept of individual rights and its application to children and parents is little more than a phantom if there is no neutral arbiter and civil authority to protect individuals and their rights and to punish those who violate them. Any discussion of rights must therefore also involve a discussion of the role played by the government in protecting the rights of individuals. How shall the government determine if a child's rights have been violated? If parents do not protect—indeed, if they violate—the rights of their children, how shall the government protect children? Short of objectively identifiable abuse, should the government have the authority to direct parents to fulfill their responsibilities and to punish them if they do not? Under what conditions should the government have the authority to take children from their parents either temporarily or permanently? Finally, how can the rights of parents be protected from the unjust actions of the government?

Generally speaking, the particular difficulties associated with identifying and defining children's rights are twofold: first, we must discern how the concept of individual rights can be applied to children who have neither the intellectual capacity to understand nor the physical means to exercise their rights; and, second, we must recognize that children's rights are to be understood and applied in the context of a separate but closely related corollary of the general doctrine of individual rights—that is, the rights of parents. Whatever rights and responsibilities children may have must be connected to and dependent upon—indeed, they must overlap and be inseparable from —the rights and responsibilities of parents and vice versa. Because the interests of children and parents are so closely linked through bonds of reciprocity, it is extremely difficult to sort out the precise boundaries. Ultimately, the challenge is to identify and define the three-way juridical relationship between parents, children, and the government.

A General Theory of Rights

In order to identify and define the rights of children and parents, we must begin with a general theory of individual rights—that is, a theory of rights that would apply universally to all human beings regardless of age. To be more precise, we need to know what rights are, where they come from, and the role they play in a civilized society. The rights of children will thus be examined as a subset or a particular instance of our broader definition of individual rights.

The conception of rights that we shall use and apply to the question of children's rights was first developed by the novelist-philosopher, Ayn Rand. Rand's unique approach to the question of rights can be seen most clearly by the way in which she defined and grounded rights. She characterized a "right" as "a moral principle defining and sanctioning a man's freedom of action in a social context."[4] Building on Rand's definition, we might say that rights are necessary principles of action to guide and protect men as they pursue life-enhancing values in a social setting. Rand viewed rights as "a moral concept—the concept that provides a logical transition from the principles guiding an individual's actions to the principles guiding his relationship with others—the concept that preserves and protects individual morality in a social context—the link between the moral code of a man and the legal code of a society, between ethics and politics."[5]

In other words, rights are moral principles that serve as a bridge between individuals and civil society. In order to live in a prosperous and civilized society, each and every man must be free to act on his judgment and the only thing that can prevent men from doing so is the initiation of physical force by other men. Rights are therefore principles of moral interaction between men in a social context; they grease the wheels of social interaction. The recognition and protection of individual rights provides the principle by which the initiation of physical force can be banned from human relationships. Thus the concept "rights" can have no meaning for a man stranded alone on a desert island.

How are rights validated or grounded? What is their source? Traditionally, rights were said to come from either God or society. By the former view, rights were said to be implanted in man by God, while as per the latter view rights were social conventions given to man as a gift. Rand rejects both views. Instead, she argues that the proper source of rights is neither divine nor congressional law, "but the law of identity" as it is applied to man's nature. In other words, rights are *discovered* principles that identify and define the "conditions of existence required by man's nature for his proper survival."[6] Man's rights are, properly defined, *objective* requirements of human life, which means that they recognize, define, and support the necessary conditions of human survival and flourishing. As such, rights consist of three interconnected, constituent elements: first, they are principles grounded on a recognition of what man is, that is, of his metaphysical nature (e.g., what he requires and must use for his survival and well-being); second, they define the conditions necessary for man to act in a social context; and, third, they sanction his freedom to act so that he may pursue those values that are necessary for him to live and live well.

The concept "rights" recognizes that it is both necessary and *right* that man be free to choose and pursue those actions that are required to support his life; that it is necessary and *right* that he keep the property he has created to support his life; and that it is necessary and *right* that he live for, benefit from, and enjoy the achievement of his highest values. Put differently, a man's life, liberty, and property are his by right. Thus a proper theory of individual rights says that man, given his nature, has a *right to life*, which means that each individual is fully sovereign over his own life and that his life is sacrosanct and cannot be harmed by another; a *right to liberty*, which means the unobstructed right to think, act, produce, and acquire values material and spiritual; a *right to property*, which means the freedom to keep, use, and dispose of the product of one's physical and mental labor; and a *right to the pursuit of happiness*, which means the freedom to choose and pursue those values that lead to one's own personal happiness. A properly defined doctrine of rights therefore establishes the moral, social, legal, and political conditions by which men can pursue the values necessary for their well-being.

The concept "rights" has a dual character: rights act as both a license and a fence. As a license, rights provide a moral and legal sanction recognizing the freedom of individuals to act in a social context in the pursuit of life-enhancing values. As a fence, rights define and erect for each and every individual defensive boundaries against the initiation of physical force. In this sense, rights establish barriers of human action between individuals in their relations with each other and between individuals in their relations with the State. If "good fences make good neighbors," as Robert Frost wrote in his poem *The Mending Wall*, so then in a moral, social and legal sense we can say "good rights make good neighbors."

In sum, the concept "rights" means freedom from the arbitrary initiation of physical force against oneself or anyone else, and it means a morally and legally recognized right or license to act in order to produce, acquire, possess, use, and trade property. Man's right (i.e., that which is the right course of action to sustain his life and achieve his values) necessitates freedom (i.e., the power to act free from the physical compulsion of other men). In other words, without freedom, there can be no rights. Right and freedom are a unity; they are necessarily connected. Thomas Jefferson made the point this way: "Liberty is unobstructed action according to our will within the limits drawn us by the equal rights of others."[7]

With a general definition of rights now established, let us examine how the principle of rights applies to children and to their parents. The rights of children and parents are a particularly vexing special instance and application of the broader concept of "rights."

The Metaphysical Basis for
the Rights of Children and Parents

To properly understand how the general concept of rights applies to children and their parents, we must first consider the metaphysical facts of reality and the specific moral conditions from which the rights and responsibilities of children and parents arise.

The first fundamental fact defining how the concept of rights applies to children and their parents is the unique moral and social context in which children are created—that is, a two-step process defined by a series of moral choices. The first step, the act of procreation resulting in the birth of a new human being, is the consequence of a *chosen* act. (Rape is an exception since the act is not mutually chosen.) Whether the parents intended to create or even ultimately wanted a child is irrelevant once the woman has given birth and the parents claim the child as theirs. The child was the foreseeable result of their mutually chosen actions. The act of procreation is therefore much more than just a physical act; it is a moral act precisely because it is a volitional act. Even more important than the choice to procreate, however, is the decision to carry a fetus to term and to bring into the world a new human being. *This* is the fundamental metaphysical fact that defines the nature of parenthood and its subsequent rights and responsibilities. This is the moment when *both* parents claim the child as theirs or give it up for adoption. A man and a woman may or may not explicitly or consciously intend to create a child, but they do absolutely choose to bring the child into the world. Whether one thinks abortion is or is not immoral and illegal is besides the point. It is simply a fact that pregnancies can be terminated whether they are illegal or not. What cannot be changed or denied, however, is that the choice to bring a child into the world creates a new series of rights and responsibilities that did not exist prior to the child's birth.

The second relevant fact crucial to identifying, defining, and sanctioning the rights of children and their parents is the unique metaphysical condition that defines childhood. This condition is characterized by three essential qualities: one, that each and every child (whether it be a newborn, a toddler, or a minor) is a metaphysically unique and distinct being; two, that children are born without any means of independent survival, which means that they are in a state of total dependence on their parents or other adults for an extended period of years; and, three, that a child's physical and mental state of being changes radically over a relatively short period of time from a state of total dependence to one of partial dependence/independence, and ultimately to a state of full self-governing independence. In sum, a newborn child is a metaphysically distinct being that is temporarily dependent on its parents or some other adults during that period of childhood in which the child's body and conceptual faculty are developing.

The Rights and Responsibilities of Parents

With these facts as our starting point, let us now examine how our general definition of rights applies to a specific kind of human relationship—the relationship between parents and their children.

Parental Property Rights in Children

The first and most important right of parents is their limited "property" right to and over *their* children.[8] This is a complex issue and no doubt a controversial claim and must therefore be explored in some detail.

Parents who have created and brought a child into the world have certain exclusive rights *to* and *over* that which they have created. A parent's proprietary right *to* their child is, in part, grounded on the fact that they have created and brought into existence this new human being. Two people—a man and a woman—have, in Lockean terms, literally mixed their labor with each other to create a new human being: a being that shares the parents' DNA. The parents have both a moral and what might be called a "genetic" investment in their child.[9] More importantly, once the fetus is brought to term and becomes an independent being through birth, that child is now legitimately claimed as the exclusive possession of its parents, unless the parents transfer their right to a third party who then becomes the child's adoptive guardian.

As we shall see, however, this property right, *unlike all other forms of property,* must be strictly limited and circumscribed by the rights of the child. This point is crucial. An individual's right to his or her children must stand alone in a category entirely different from all other forms of property, including the property right to their house, their land, their car, or their pets. Children are not and cannot be owned or treated, unlike other forms of personal property, as though they were chattel. The legal status of children relative to other forms of property must be recognized as a totally separate category under the law. In ways limited and circumscribed by the child's fundamental right to life, parents do, however, claim an exclusive dominion to control and direct the affairs of their children as minors.

A parent's right to and over his child is defined morally and legally by exclusivity. A newborn child belongs exclusively to one set of parents and to no other. This first and fundamental right bars any third party—including the State—from claiming the child as its own and seizing it by force. The doctrine of the State as parens patriae relative to children is, as we shall see, fundamentally totalitarian in nature and therefore hostile to the principles and practice of a free and just society.[10] Children belong to their parents and not to the State.

As creators of the child ex nihilo, there is a very real sense in which parents have a limited liberty right and therefore a limited property right—limited in duration and scope—to that which they have created. Let us be clear in what we mean here. Parental rights must be understood contextually. The ownership claim of a parent is *relative* in relation to the child given that the child is also a rights-bearing person, but it is *absolute* in relation to third parties. In this sense, the right of a parent to their child serves as a fence protecting the parents' right against any form of child stealing. No third party can assert a claim to someone else's child.

Our point is illustrated through the following simple but all-too-real scenario. If a government official from the Department of Social Services accompanied by an armed police officer were to turn up at your home unannounced and with no justifiable cause, knock on the door, and say, "We've come to take your children, turn them over," it is entirely natural and proper for you to reject their demand by saying: "No, you can't have them; they're *my* children." Significantly, common everyday experience tells us that virtually all parents (and probably even most childless adults) would respond to such a command with exactly these same or similar words. In a very real and proper sense, your children are indeed yours and no one else's, but what virtually all parents lack is a proper philosophic understanding of what it means to say "they're *my* children." Parents should claim this right as an *absolute* vis-à-vis all other parties as long as they do not act in such a way so as to violate the child's own rights.[11] Ultimately, the deepest purpose of this chapter is to explain what it means for parents to say in ordinary language, "they're *my* children," that is, to give voice to a universally accepted but hitherto unarticulated moral claim.

Parental Property Rights over Their Children

How does the parent's property-claim stand relative to the child's? The nature of the parents' rights must now be viewed from a different perspective. The right no longer serves as a fence as it did relative to all third parties, but instead it now serves as a license giving the parents the freedom to act in a certain context—a context defined by both the interests and rights of the child.

The rights and discretionary authority of parents over *their* children are and must be quite broad. The parents' prerogative authority over their children is defined by the fact that infants, toddlers, and young children do not have the means to survive on their own. They are completely dependent on their parents or guardians for their survival. Parents therefore have a right to determine how they will fulfill their responsibility to nourish and protect their children.

As a corollary to their right to determine how they will provide sustenance for their children, parents also have the right to restrict the actions of their children in all kinds of ways and the right to compel them to act in various ways. Parents have a right and an obligation to control and regulate the freedom of their children. In fact, parents have a limited right to use coercion against their children in order to prevent some harm to the child or to bring about some good for the child. Parents regularly and properly regulate the child's freedom of action in all kinds of ways. Children are "forced" by their parents to do many things they do not want to do (e.g., going to bed), and they are prevented from doing many things they want to do (e.g., playing on the street). Parents of infants, toddlers, and young children use this kind of benevolent coercion every single day virtually from the moment the child wakes up in the morning to the time when they go to sleep at night.

This parental right to limit their child's freedom extends to a limitless variety of optional values. Parents control what their children can and cannot do. For instance, parents have a right to dictate what, when, where, and how a baby, a toddler, or a young child will eat, dress, or play, what books they shall read, and which movies they shall watch. They have a right to control what, when, where, and with whom they will associate. As their children get older, parents have a right to dictate how a child is to be educated morally and intellectually, what sports the child will or will not play, and the kind of music they will listen to in the parents' home. If the parent says "you shall only listen to classical music in our home" or "you shall only listen to jazz or bagpipe music in our home," the child must accede to the wishes of the parents.

It is not the case, however, that parents have an absolute, arbitrary, or unlimited power over their children to do with them as they please. A parent's guardianship and temporary jurisdiction over their child is not and must never be absolute or tyrannical. Parental rights (as well as those of children) must be understood contextually: they are absolute in a certain context and relative or conditional in another. A parent's right to and over their child is *absolute* relative to the State and to other individuals so long as the parent does not violate the rights of the child. The parents' right to and over their child is, however, *relative* to the child and its nature (i.e., to the child's rapidly changing physical and cognitive context and to the child's rights). A parent has a right to limit the child's liberty in all sorts of ways, but they may not limit or violate the child's right to life. Furthermore, a parent's right to direct and limit a toddler's freedom of action is, for instance, virtually all encompassing when it is six months old but diminishes over time relative to the cognitive and moral growth of the child. A parent's right to and over their child does not and must not, however, include the right to physically or cognitively abuse a child. Parents may not inflict lasting physical damage to a child (e.g., maiming or mutilating), nor may they cripple or damage a child's cognitive faculties.

In sum, the child's right to life stands paramount against the parents' property right in their child. Parental control of their children is thus limited in both time and scope by virtue of the fact that the children are rights-bearers themselves. In this regard, parents can only claim *temporarily* (i.e., until a defined age of majority) and in a defined and *limited* context (i.e., relative to the rights of the child) the child as a possession relative to all other third parties but a possession of a very peculiar kind, one that bears rights of its own. Put somewhat differently, it may be more appropriate to say that parents assume a kind of temporary but conditionally absolute guardianship or jurisdictional authority over their children. To be more precise, the parents have a right—a property right—to be the guardians of the child's rights. They are the first line of defense in protecting the child's right to life. Should the parents fail to protect, or, worse, should they infringe upon the child's right to life, the parents' property right in the child is forfeited and may be ceded to or assumed by the government.[12]

As a result of having a right to their children, parents also have certain jurisdictional rights *over* their children, which means that they have a right to raise their children according to their values without the interference of other individuals or the State. This is especially true with regard to education. In a properly constructed individual-rights republic, parents can expect and demand from their neighbors or the government a large sphere of freedom of action and noninterference when it comes to raising and educating their children. Individuals will and do disagree about how to feed, clothe, shelter, and educate children, but no one—including the State—has a right to force parents to raise their children in a manner of which the parents disapprove. In a free society that respects the rights of individuals, the government cannot and should not force its particular conception of the "good" on parents and their children. Education must be the special preserve of parents and, ultimately, over time, of the child himself. American courts, and the U.S. Supreme Court in particular, have deemed a parent's right to make decisions concerning the care, custody, and education of one's children a fundamental right deserving of "heightened protection against government interference."[13]

Consider what it would mean to deny parents the fundamental right to educate their children on the grounds that the State has a right to ensure that all children are educated according to State standards. Imagine, for instance, a married couple who not only homeschool their children but give them a world-class education by virtually any standard. Imagine further that the parents refuse to provide the State with documentation of what and how their children are being educated on the grounds that the State has no moral right to monitor, control, or regulate how the child is being educated. How should the State treat such parents? Under these circumstances, does the State have a compelling interest to arrest and imprison the parents and to put the children in foster care under its truancy laws? The answer must be "no," at least not if you choose to live in a free society that recognizes and respects the rights of parents to *their* children.

In a free and just society, parents must have the right to educate their children without any supervision or oversight from the State. It would be a gross violation of the parents' rights for the State to attempt to enter the home or, worse yet, to remove a child from a home because the State does not approve of certain kinds of education. That a small fraction of parents might not properly educate their children according to "community standards" does not justify the State violating the rights of those parents who are educating their children.[14]

But when or how shall the rights of children be protected when parents demonstrably violate them? If parents fail to protect their child's right to life—indeed, if they demonstrably abuse their children physically or cognitively—the State does then have a compelling claim to serve as the agent-protector of the child's rights. Generally speaking, though, the State's role vis-à-vis children—indeed, its only role—must be strictly negative (as it is with adults): it is to protect children from objectively demonstrable abuse, that is, from a violation of the child's right to grow into a rational, self-governing individual. The State cannot force parents to feed their children certain kinds of foods, dress them in certain kinds of clothes, shelter them in certain kinds of domiciles, or educate them in a particular way, but it can remove children from homes where they are being starved or maimed, or where they are being abused cognitively. Parents have a right to feed their children broccoli against the child's cries of disgust or red meat against the howls of People for the Ethical Treatment of Animals, but they do not have a right to feed their children poison.

Parental Responsibilities

Parents, in addition to having rights to and over their children, also have moral and legal responsibilities connected to their rights.

Because they have created and chosen to bring into the world a new human being and because that child is initially in a state of total dependency, parents must accept and fulfill certain obligations—chosen obligations—to their child. The moral responsibilities of parenthood are among the most important and challenging obligations that individuals can assume in a lifetime. Parents have a responsibility to their children that can, under certain limited and defined circumstances, be enforced by the State, that is, to ensure that the child is not denied the physical and mental means or ability to live and to achieve *some* "good" over time—a "good" ultimately chosen by the child.[15]

From whence derives this responsibility, and what, if anything, should happen to those parents who do not fulfill their parental responsibilities? The proper lens through which to view the unique relationship between parents and children, the means by which to sort out their mutually reinforcing rights and responsibilities, is the language of contracts. By virtue of their choice to create and give birth to a new human being and given the *nature* of their creation (i.e., a dependent, rights-bearing being), parents enter into a tacit *moral* agreement with each other by which they assume the responsibility to sustain, nurture, protect, and educate their child into adulthood. The right to create in this context does not, however, include the right to destroy or maim in the same way that a property owner can destroy a house that he has built. Indeed, quite the opposite is true. By choosing to create and bring a child into the world, parents assume certain fiduciary obligations that are analogous to a particular kind of contract recognized in law: third-party beneficiary contracts.[16] As third-party beneficiaries, children are not a party to the contract, but they are the intended beneficiary of the contract. In order for the parents' limited property right to their child to be recognized and protected by the government, they must also enter into a tacit *legal* agreement with the government, the purpose of which is to guarantee the parents' exclusive ownership claim to their children in exchange for a promise to sustain and nourish (physically and cognitively) for a limited time that which they have created (i.e., a rights-bearing being).[17]

The primary responsibility of parents is to provide their children with the physical and mental sustenance necessary to become self-governing adults. In addition to feeding and protecting their children, parents have an obligation to ensure that their children reach the conceptual level of human development.[18] The paramount parental objective should be to provide the necessary means by which the children will gradually grow into rational, independent, responsible, and productive adults. Parents therefore have a moral and a legal obligation to sustain and nourish the bodies and minds of their children—which means to feed, clothe and protect their progeny; to facilitate the development of their rational faculties; as well as to provide them with some kind of education so that they can earn a livelihood as adults. Ultimately, the primary responsibility of parents is to provide their children with a home environment that is benevolent and rational—one that equips the children to act on their own judgment so that they can eventually govern themselves. This means that parents have a moral responsibility to provide their children with, at the very least, some minimal education so that they can live as rational, rights-respecting adults.

The parent–child relationship and the tacit contract that binds it together also evolve over the course of time. At first, the parents bear full responsibility for the child's well-being and the child owes its parents nothing morally. In legal terms, if the parents default on their tacit contract with their child—if they refuse to provide the child with the means to life—if in effect they commit not only criminal *fraud* but assault and battery or worse, the State then should have the authority to serve as the child's representative or agent. The State has the right to protect children from abusive or criminally negligent parents, and it can represent the child in a suit against the parents for a violation of the child's rights.[19] Over time, however, parental responsibilities recede and the responsibilities of children increase—responsibilities for their own well-being and responsibilities to respect the property rights of their parents (e.g., the parent who tells his daughter, "if you live in my home, you need to be in the house by 11:00 P.M."). The child's right to life therefore must be protected by the State if the parents fail to ensure it.

The Rights and Responsibilities of Children

Let us now consider how the concept of individual rights applies directly to children. This is, obviously, a very complicated and specialized issue in the philosophy of law because the rights of children are intimately intertwined with the equally complicated question of parental rights, and because children do not have the qualities necessary to know and therewith to exercise the full rights of adults.

The Special and Complex Nature of Children's Rights

The rights of children are a special instance of and, in many ways, an exception to the concept of rights as it applies to adults. We can see the difficult nature of this issue by simply stating what rights children have and do not have. Like adults, children have an absolute right to life, but unlike adults they do not have the corollary rights to liberty, property, or the pursuit of happiness, at least not as infants, toddlers, and young children. These corollary rights apply only to fully rational beings. A child's liberty can and almost certainly must be restricted, for instance, by a limited form of physical coercion. In fact, as any parent or guardian knows, a good deal of one's time is spent monitoring, controlling, restricting, and guiding how infants, toddlers, and young children use their liberty. Parents and guardians initiate what we might call soft or benevolent coercion on their children virtually every day, all day. In this way, parents are actually educating their children for the rights-based liberty that comes with adulthood. Until that time, however, children exercise and enjoy these corollary rights vicariously through their parents.

Likewise, given their unique metaphysical condition, the nature of a child's right to life is both similar to and different from an adult's right to life. Like all adults, children have a right to life, which means that their lives may not be destroyed or maimed by another human being. Unlike adults, however, children do have a rights-claim against their parents to be fed, clothed, and sheltered. In other words, given their unique metaphysical status, a child's right to life is more expansive than that of adults. For example, children have some rights that adults do not have (e.g., the right to be fed, clothed, sheltered, and minimally educated), but they do not have some rights that adults do have (e.g., the right to liberty or property). Let us now work through the apparent complications of this difficult issue.

With the birth of a child an amalgam of interconnected rights is created. As with adults, each and every child is a metaphysically distinct and unique being that is born with rights that merit protection (i.e., principally the right to life). This means, for instance, that children, like adults, have a moral and a legal right to life—that is, the right to live and develop into an adult—that must not be violated by the initiation of physical force. For anyone—including a parent—to kill a child is to commit a homicide in the very same way that to murder an adult is a homicide legally punishable by the government. Given the manner in which the child was created and brought into the world (i.e., by a volitional act of two adults) and given the child's unique metaphysical status (i.e., his complete dependence on adults for survival), the child's right to life is held as a trusteeship by the parents. The child is their creation (in whom they hold a limited property right), the child cannot exist without the support of the parents (or surrogate parents), and therefore the parents have a moral and a legal responsibility to support the child's life. If the parents refuse to support the child or if they are unable to do it, they then lose either permanently or temporarily their right to their child.

But when we say that a child has a right to life, what exactly does this mean in moral and legal terms? How does a moral right translate into a legal right that requires protection by the government? Consider, for instance, how the law does and should respect a child's right to life vis-à-vis their parents. Parents or guardians who intentionally starve a child or who don't provide him with the proper clothing or shelter necessary for survival despite having the means to do so are guilty not only of a moral crime but of having violated the child's right to life. Likewise, if the parents through negligence do not provide sufficient food, clothing, or shelter to sustain the child's physical well-being, they are guilty of a moral crime as well as some form of criminal negligence. But if the parents are incapable of providing for the physical well-being of their child through no fault of their own (e.g., a plague or famine, or the long-term or catastrophic illness or injury of one or both parents), the family's situation should be judged as tragic, as the parents have committed neither a moral nor a legal crime. In all three instances, however, the government (under the appropriate conditions and with the proper resources) must have the legal authority to protect the child's right to life, rescue him from an impending death or physical harm and place him with welcoming relatives, in a foster home, or with some charitable organization. The same principle would also apply to parents who refuse to allow their children proper medical care that would save their lives. In those cases where parents have intentionally or through negligence abused a child, they should be punished and required to pay for the upkeep of their child.

The moral principle of a "right to life" is, as it applies to children, a much broader concept than it is for adults. A child's right to life extends beyond his physical existence; it includes the development of his rational faculty. There is no life for adults without the use of the mind. Because reason is man's basic tool of survival, children do have a moral claim and, implicitly, a contractual right as a third-party beneficiary to be provided by their parents or guardians with the necessary physiological and cognitive means required for the normal development of their rational faculty. In the same way that parents have a moral and legal obligation to provide for the physical sustenance of their children, so they must provide their children with the intellectual sustenance necessary to become eventually self-governing and self-reliant individuals.

How, then, would a child's right to life be violated as it relates to their cognitive development? In other words, what constitutes cognitive child abuse? Just in the same way that it would be a violation of a child's rights to abuse him physically, so too would it be a violation of the child's rights to subject him to cognitive or mental abuse. It would, for instance, be a violation of a child's rights to be locked in a room for extended periods of time deprived of sunlight and sensory and mental stimulation. To deny a child the ability to learn a language would also be a form of abuse as it would do permanent and irreparable damage to the child's potential cognitive development and therewith their ability to acquire any language as an adult. Such actions are a breach of the child's third-party contractual rights vis-à-vis their parents. Consider, for instance, the case of feral children whose cognitive development has been dwarfed intentionally and permanently by their parents. It would *not*, however, be a violation of a child's right to not receive a certain kind of education. A child does not have an inalienable right to learn Latin or calculus or to receive the latest form of "diversity" training. Indeed, children do not have a right *to* an education per se, but more on this anon.

The Evolving Nature of Children's Rights

The subject of children's rights is made interesting and challenging by virtue of the fact that a child's metaphysical state of being changes quite profoundly over the course of a few years. Newborn children come into the world devoid not only of any knowledge but even of a neurologically developed conceptual faculty. Although the infant has the potential to develop the power of reason (the power distinguishing man from all other animals), he does not yet have it. His faculties are undeveloped and only a potential. But unlike the newborn of all other animal species, human babies are born tabula rasa and do not have any natural instincts to help them survive. The long-term survival and flourishing of every child requires that its conceptual faculty be developed and exercised under some kind of deliberate and supervised guidance.

To become fully human—to become self-governing—*is* to develop the rational faculty, which means that the process required for developing the child's mental faculties is a critically important element in the process of maturation from infant to child to adult. At first, the child is utterly helpless and completely dependent. Not until the child has begun to develop his conceptual faculty can he act responsibly and in his self-interest. This process takes several years. The natural condition of children is to evolve from a state of total dependence to a state of partial dependence and ultimately to a state of self-governing independence. Until that time, though, until the child grows physically and cognitively and can assume "actual" self-governance, he is under the "virtual" proprietorship of his parents or guardians, who have a kind of fiduciary power over and responsibility to the child.

It is only through the development of the conceptual faculty over the course of a 10- or a 12-year period that the child becomes a full rights-bearing, rights-respecting individual. And as a child's metaphysical condition changes, so does the status of his rights. The concept of rights cannot apply to a six-month-old infant in the same way that it applies to a six-year-old child or a 16-year-old teenager. Rights are and must be, in the full sense of the term, connected primarily to rationality, to one's volitional capacity, and to one's ability for self-government. Thus the sphere of children's rights and responsibilities (i.e., their freedom of action) expands gradually over time. As they mature, as their cognitive faculty develops, and as they gain control and authority over their own thoughts and actions, the sphere of liberty and responsibility granted to children expands. A two-year-old will not understand the nature and meaning of liberty, property, contracts or the pursuit of happiness, but a 12-year-old could begin to do so. Children do therefore have individual rights above and beyond the absolute right to life, which they have from the moment of birth, but those corollary rights—that is, the rights of individuals such as liberty, property and the pursuit of happiness—are held and manifested in a way somewhat different from those of adults.

Children are, we might say, proto-rights bearers. Their rights are in effect held in trust temporarily by their parents or guardians. This is why society also applies criminal, contract, and tort law differently to children than it does to adults. Young children cannot make legally binding contracts, for instance, without the consent of their parents. Eventually, however, as their rational faculties develop and as they become more capable of governing themselves over time, children begin to assume the rights that have been held in trust for them by their parents and society, and at the same time the obligations owed to them by their parents recede accordingly.

Given the distinctive metaphysical condition of children, the concept of rights—and especially the right to life—applies differently to them than it does to adults. From the time that children are born and for several years afterward, they are in a state of total dependence on their parents. Newborns and infants require therefore the positive action of their parents or some adult in order for them to survive and to develop physically and mentally. During this state of helplessness and dependence, the child does have a right to life—indeed, a rather expansive right to life—that must be ensured by the child's parents, and with that right comes certain contractual rights or entitlements that apply *only* to children relative to their parents. The child does have a contractual rights-claim to be fed, clothed, protected, and educated (in some minimal way) by their parents. They don't have a right to be fed caviar, to wear Gucci shoes, or to be educated at Choate, but they do have a right to be fed, clothed, and protected in order to ensure their right to life, and they have a right to a minimal education (e.g., to learn a language) that will allow them one day to be rights-bearing and rights-respecting adults.

The status of children's rights, particularly newborns, infants, and small children, can be thought of as the obverse of those of adults. For adults, rights represent a moral and a legal fence that prevents other individuals from invading their freedom of thought and action and vice versa. Children, in a slightly more limited context, do have the same right to noninterference held by adults. It would, as we have already seen, be a rights violation for anyone, including a child's parents, to murder, maim, or abuse a child physically. But children do, given their metaphysical status as dependents and given that they did not ask to be created in order to be abused, have certain limited contractual rights-claims as third-party beneficiaries *to* things that must be provided for them by those who created them or by their legal guardians. They are and must be the constant beneficiaries of care from their parents or guardians. A child's right to life means, therefore, in a limited sense, that it has a contractual right to be fed, to be clothed, and to be protected by its parents.

But these rights-claims, however, should only be morally and legally specific to, and valid against, the child's parents or legal guardians. The obligation and the right are entirely personal and limited in the same way that a contract between two individuals is limited to the contracting parties. A parent who abuses or does not satisfy his fiduciary obligations to his children may be said, under certain circumstances, to have forfeited his right to his children (either temporarily or permanently, depending on the severity of the rights violation). Such a parent has committed a form of criminal fraud. There is a sense in which we can say that a parent has initiated force against their child if they do not provide the child with the necessities of life in the same way that fraud and extortion involve the indirect use of force. Thus the government in a free society does have the authority to protect children and to prosecute parents for parental malfeasance.

It is important to note therefore that these rights are meaningful only in the context of the child's relationship to his parent; they are specifically connected to the obligations of the child's parent. A child does *not* have a right to be fed, clothed, protected, and educated by individuals other than his parents until or unless the parents fail to perform their responsibility. A child's right to physical and intellectual sustenance is not a universal rights-claim against "society," but is rather a right connected to particular individuals in the same way that an individual owed a debt from a particular individual has no claim on society as a whole to satisfy the debt. There can be no right, including those of children, to violate the rights of others. The "right" to infringe the rights of others is a contradiction in terms.

A Child's Right to an Education

And now, finally, let us turn directly to the more difficult question of a child's right to an education. It should be clear by now that children do not have a general right to an education in the way that many people today speak of rights. Children do not have a rights-claim against society to be educated. That said, it is true that parents clearly have a moral responsibility to provide their children with some kind of an education in the same way that they have an obligation to feed, clothe, and shelter them, and it is also true that children have some limited right to be educated by their parents. Defining how this right ought to be protected, though, is a difficult task. It would clearly be a form of cognitive abuse and therefore a rights violation for a child to be locked in a room for weeks, months, or years, preventing them from developing their conceptual faculty. Such action by the parents would be a criminal rights violation that would require the State to act as the child's protector-agent and to rescue him and place him in some kind of protective care. But it would not be a violation of a child's contractual right to be educated by his parents if the parents did not provide their child with a formal academic education but instead provided him with an education in a particular kind of work (e.g., as a fisherman in Alaska or as a rancher in Texas). Nor would it be a violation of the child's contractual rights if the parents were homeschooling "unschoolers," who choose not to teach their children how to read until the children show an interest in learning how to read. Some "unschooled" children, for instance, do not learn to read until after they are the age of 10 or 12, but surely we would not say that their moral right to be educated had been violated and that the State should swoop in and save them.[20]

The State cannot and should not be involved in defining what constitutes a "good" education. The State's only legitimate role is to protect individuals from objectively identifiable rights' violations. In the end, we draw this conclusion: In a free society, the State should play *no* role in the education of children; that is, there should be a complete separation of school and State. The role of the State should be strictly limited to protecting the rights of individuals, which can and sometimes will include protecting the rights of children from cognitive child abuse. Otherwise, parents should be left free to provide for the education of their children.

As we have seen, the application of the concept of individual rights to children is a difficult subject. Describing the precise conditions and drawing the exact boundaries of the parent–child relationship and the role that the State should play in protecting children should probably be left in theory to those who work in the philosophy of law and in practice to common law courts. Still, as difficult and as emotionally charged as this issue may be for some people, we must keep in mind that in a free and just society this would be a marginal issue. It is possible that in a free society (one that respects and protects individual rights), a very small percentage of children might not receive a good education (which would be a tragedy), but such a society would still be moral and just and the quality of education for most children would almost certainly improve dramatically. Contemporary experience and history demonstrate that virtually all parents in a free society will take full responsibility for the education of their children (in varying degrees, of course) in the same way that they care for their physical health. Contrast that with a society that does not respect and protect individual rights in the name of a universal "right" to an education. The result is a society that is both immoral and unjust and that also fails to educate most children on a daily basis. We should not be surprised that a moral and just system leads to good results while an immoral and unjust system leads to bad results.

The conclusion before us is now obvious. A free, moral, and just society is one in which all individuals shall have the right and shall assume the responsibility for educating their own children.

Notes

1. I would like to thank Eric Allison, Andrew Bernstein, Thomas Bowden, Jenn Casey, Daniel R. Chalykoff, Henry Clark, George Clowes, Eric Daniels, Diana Hsieh, Adam Mossoff, James Otteson, and Brandon Turner for reading this chapter and for offering many thoughtful suggestions for improving it. I would also like to thank Chris Tollefsen for asking the question that first inspired the writing of this chapter.

2. For the UN Universal Declaration of Human Rights, see http://www.un.org /en/documents/udhr/index.shtml.

3. Each state government in the United States is required by its constitution to provide a school system for its children, which is to say that the right to an education is virtually universally accepted in this country. Interestingly, though, the Supreme Court of the United States in *San Antonio Independent School District v. Rodriguez* (1973) rejected the claim that education is a "right" recognized by the constitution of the United States.

4. Ayn Rand, "Man's Rights," in *The Virtue of Selfishness* (New York: Signet, 1961), 110. For a more fully developed academic presentation of Rand's theory of rights, see Tara Smith, *Moral Rights and Political Freedom* (Lanham, MD: Rowman & Littlefield, 1995).

5. Rand, "Man's Rights," in *The Virtue of Selfishness* (New York: Signet, 1961), p. 108.

6. Ibid., p. 111.

7. Thomas Jefferson to Isaac Tiffany, April 4, 1819, in *Jefferson: Political Writings*, eds., Joyce Appleby and Terrence Ball (Cambridge: Cambridge University Press, 1999), 224.

8. The parents' limited property right to and over their child has been recognized in America's judicial courts. See *Turner v. Turner,* 167 334 P.2d 1011 (Cal.App. 1959), where the court held "The right of a fit and proper parent to his child's custody is somewhat in the nature of a property right, and is paramount, in a sense, to the child's theoretical welfare and best interests. *Shea v. Shea*, 100 Cal.App.2d 60, 65, 223 P.2d 32. A parent entitled to the custody of a child has a right to change his residence. Civ. Code, § 213. The parents are the natural guardians of their child, and are responsible to the state for the child's well-being. 37 Cal.Jur.2d 145, § 7. The parent has authority to control the child, and to administer restraint and punishment, in order to compel obedience to reasonable and necessary directions. *People v. Curtiss*, 116 Cal.App.Supp. 771, 300 P. 801."

9. I thank my colleague Henry Clark for bringing the concept "genetic investment" to my attention.

10. Parens patriae is generally defined as "the state as parent."

11. Third parties should have the moral authority and right to intervene in the relationship between parents and their children in order to protect a child from legally defined physical abuse. Law-making bodies and/or courts would be responsible for defining criminal assault in the case of children. The Supreme Court of the United States addressed this issue in *Santosky v. Kramer* 455 U.S. 745 (1982). Writing for the Court, Justice Blackmun opined, "The fundamental liberty interest of natural parents in the care, custody, and management of their child does not evaporate simply because they have not been model parents or have lost temporary custody of their child to the State. Even when blood relationships are

strained, parents retain a vital interest in preventing the irretrievable destruction of their family life. If anything, persons faced with forced dissolution of their parental rights have a more critical need for procedural protections than do those resisting state intervention into ongoing family affairs. When the State moves to [p754] destroy weakened familial bonds, it must provide the parents with fundamentally fair procedures."

12. Parenthood should be thought of as a separate category in the law distinguished from guardianship or trusteeship.

13. See *Meyer v. Nebraska*, 262 U.S. (1923) or *Washington v. Glucksberg* (1997).

14. Consider, for instance, the case of John Singer. Singer, a Mormon, was killed during a standoff in 1979 by Utah law enforcement officials who were attempting to arrest him for homeschooling his children. The facts of the Singer case are told in Carl Watner "Who Controls the Children?" in *Homeschooling: A Hope for America*, ed. Carl Watner (Gramling, SC: The Voluntaryists, 2010), p. 60–73.

15. I reject the claim of the libertarian intellectual Murray Rothbard, who argues that "a parent does not have the right to aggress against his child," but then goes on to argue that a parent "should not have a *legal obligation* to feed, clothe, or educate his children, since such obligations would entail positive acts coerced upon the parent and depriving the parent of his rights." According to Rothbard, a parent "should have the legal right *not* to feed the child, i.e., to allow it to die." See Rothbard, *The Ethics of Liberty* (New York: New York University Press, 2002), p. 100.

16. On third-party beneficiary contracts, see Jan Hallebeek and Harry Dondorp, eds., *Contracts for a Third-Party Beneficiary: A Historical and Comparative Account* (Leiden, The Netherlands: Martinus Nijhoff Publishers, 2008); Vernon V. Palmer, *The Paths to Privity: The History of Third Party Beneficiary Contracts at English Law* (Clark, NJ: Lawbook Exchange, 2006). I would like to recognize and thank Professor Adam Mossoff of the George Mason School of Law for bringing to my attention the legal doctrine of third-party beneficiary contracts and its potential application to the relationship between parents and children.

17. This agreement begins when the parents seek from the government a sanction for their right in the form of a birth certificate.

18. For an excellent treatment of what we mean in suggesting that parents have a moral–legal responsibility to ensure that they reach the conceptual level of cognition, see Ayn Rand's essay "The Comprachicos," in *The Return of the Primitive: The Anti-industrial Revolution* (New York: Penguin, 1999), pp. 51–95.

19. By the same token, as a moral–legal matter, parents (and taxpayers) should have the right to sue the government whenever it fraudulently defaults on its "contract" to educate their children.

20. Consider, for instance, the case of unschooled children who did not learn to read until they were ten years old, but then went on to matriculate from Harvard and other Ivy League universities. For a small sampling of such stories, see http://www.singlearticles.com/is-this-any-way-a785.html, or http://www.thecrimson.com/article/2006/4/17/homeschoolers-a-small-but-growing-minority/, or http://www.denverpost.com/ci_8385957.

Chapter 8

Universal Choice or Bust!

Greg Forster

I've been toiling in the trenches of education reform for nine years—
not as long as most of the other contributors to this volume, but long
enough. I've done work on accountability testing, merit pay, class
size reduction, alternative teacher training, desegregation, school
finance, special education, dropout rates, college readiness, charter
schools, tax credits, and vouchers. Looking back, and surveying the
landscape we're working in now, I've come to a conclusion.

In most circumstances, marginal education reforms aren't worth
the investment. There are exceptions, when circumstances happen
to converge in a way that makes incremental improvements cost-
effective. But on the whole, if the complete breaking of the government monopoly—which is another way of saying the enactment of
universal school choice—is something that can never happen in a
million years, then more incremental education reforms are almost
never worth the trouble they cost, and most of us reformers should
go do something else with our lives. And shame on us for wasting
our time on schools when there are policy problems out there that
are actually fixable.

But if universal choice can happen, then no other political cause
is more worth fighting for. No other public policy reform has anything like the potential of universal school choice to radically transform not only schools but all of American society for the better.

The promise of America is that no one will be held back from
reaching his or her full potential by the coercive exploitation of the
powerful. That promise has never been fully realized, of course.

From the beginning, the powerful have found numerous ways to exploit the weak in America, in spite of the promise that lies at the heart of our national experience.

But the promise endures, and each generation of Americans is called to claim it and work to make it more fully real. In our generation, breaking the public school monopoly is by far the most urgent political task before us if we are serious about answering the call to make the promise of America a reality.

And, paradoxically, if universal choice can happen, then some of the less-ambitious reforms are also worth fighting for—if they move us toward that goal. There isn't much point to investing in anything other than radical victory, meaning the end of the education monopoly. But there are some marginal reforms that can help us get there, provided we keep our eye on the ball. We must ruthlessly narrow down our efforts and support only those reforms that truly do help us get to universal choice, rather than dissipating our resources of time, money, and energy by promoting every program that's labeled "school choice."

My mentor and dear friend Jay P. Greene opens this volume with an appeal that we not let the perfect be the enemy of the good. He urges us to embrace marginal reforms that do some good rather than keep our strength in reserve, waiting for a major upheaval in education policy that may never come.

I'm not ashamed to say that Jay taught me pretty much everything I know about education reform. And I'm sympathetic to his concerns here.

There's an old story about a socialist professor and his graduate student who pass a beggar while walking down the street. The student reaches into his pocket to get some money to give to the beggar, but the professor slaps his hand away: "Don't delay the revolution!"

I don't want to be that professor. Nonetheless, considering the strategic needs of the school choice movement, I must offer the following dissent.

Or perhaps it's not so much a dissent as a paradoxical corollary. Let's call it Greene's Law that our desire to achieve radical victory should not inhibit us from pursuing cost-effective marginal reforms. I offer Forster's Corollary: marginal reforms are almost never cost-effective except when they produce substantial movement toward radical victory.

Why the Schools Aren't Fixed Yet

There's no getting around it: the obstacles to any type of education reform are daunting. It takes a lot of blood, sweat, and tears to wrest any real change from the death grip of the teachers' unions, the staff unions, the education schools, the administrators' associations, and all the rest of the extensive apparatus of oppression and ruin that we know as "the blob." It doesn't matter if you're talking about testing, pay, tenure, parent choice, or any other type of reform. To get any policy change that delivers serious improvement of the system, you have to pay dearly.

The blob has billion-dollar budgets and an army of thousands of volunteer workers that reaches into every city block, suburban development, and rural village across the country. Probably even more important than that, though, is the nature of the beast itself. When we face the unions and their allies, we are up against people who make their living by destroying children's lives. They are ruthless and will stop at nothing to fight us off.

Everyone can see how this makes it difficult to obtain an education reform. Not everyone sees how this makes implementing and sustaining reforms after you first "obtain" them not just difficult but usually impossible.

Examples that illustrate this point are legion. They run from the "vocational education" programs that were so popular in the first half of this century, which ended up mainly as an excuse to warehouse minority students without teaching them, all the way to the failure of No Child Left Behind to produce any meaningful improvement in results. Indeed, the history of K-12 education in the twentieth century—especially since the rise of unionization—consists almost entirely of such examples.

The pattern is easily recognizable to anyone who knows the history. First there will be a major public alarm that the education system is broken. Then there will be a major reform movement. Then the blob will fight off most of the really useful ideas, but a few of the movement's policies will actually be adopted. Then the popular alarm will die down and the political capital supporting the reform will evaporate. Then the blob will frustrate the implementation of the new policy, or get to work co-opting it and turning it into something else. The outcome is always the same—the system doesn't change, and another generation of students loses the opportunity for a better education. When this gets noticed, the next public alarm starts and we're right back on the merry-go-round.

In fact, as I write, we're in the process of going through all this once again with national—excuse me, "common"—education outcome standards. The president announced that states "voluntarily" adopting common standards would be favored for new education subsidies, and publicly hinted that maybe, perhaps, recalcitrant states would lose their Title I funding. Wham, a "voluntary" common standards system materialized out of nowhere. Some conservatives, liking the sound of "standards," climbed on board. But even as the final nails were being hammered into the frame for national standards, the U.S. Department of Education—blob central—was already moving to take them over by sponsoring the creation of "assessment systems" to accompany the standards. Once national standards exist, how do we keep them from being captured by the blob and used to promote everything from fuzzy math to socialist realism? Conservative advocates had no answer to that question, because there can be none.[1]

Meanwhile, at the time of this writing DC Mayor Adrian Fenty has just lost his party primary to a race-hustling hack who's deeply in hock to the blob. Nationally celebrated reformer Michelle Rhee is on track to get unceremoniously sacked, with all her famous victories expected to be undone the moment she's out the door. The math is pretty simple: the more successful Rhee was, the more incentive the unions had to invest in destroying her.

The lack of results from decades of going round and round on this carnival ride is clear from the National Assessment of Educational Progress (NAEP). From when NAEP was created in 1971 to the most recent test in 2008, the nation's 17-year-olds went from 306 to 308 in math and from 285 to 286 in reading. That's a change of two points and one point respectively, on a scale of 500 points.[2]

We don't have reliable ways to measure learning outcomes across the whole population before NAEP was created, but I don't know of anyone who thinks we're doing better now than we were doing before 1971. And the various excuses that are offered for the lack of progress don't hold any water.[3]

The other major measurement of success, high school graduation, is also flat. The best measurement we have of graduation rates before recent years is the number of graduates divided by the number of 17-year-olds. That rate steadily climbed to its all-time peak in 1970 at 77 percent, then just as steadily declined until it bottomed out at 67.5 percent in 1998, before climbing back to 75 percent in 2008.[4] Actually, that's worse than flat—the rate went down and then came back up to where it had been. "Flat" would have been a whole lot better!

There have been a few exceptions. Florida's spectacularly successful "A+" reform program, implemented in 1998—combining vouchers, an end to social promotion, and school-level accountability for student learning gains—is the most notable. The comprehensive reform of instructional standards in Massachusetts in the 1990s is another.

Yet these exceptions were the result of rare combinations of circumstances. Unusually strong public support for reform was combined with an unusually strong presence of reformers in key positions of influence, as well as other factors.

It is particularly telling that no other state followed in their footsteps. What other state adopted governance reforms on anything like the level of Florida's? Or standards reforms on anything like the level of Massachusetts'? Under ordinary circumstances, reforms like these don't happen.

And even these exceptional victories are turning out to be fragile. The voucher component of Florida's school reforms was struck down in a bizarre, self-contradictory, and inaccuracy-laden decision by the state's supreme court in 2006. And Deval Patrick began dismantling key elements of Massachusetts' reforms after he was elected governor in the same year, a process that continued throughout his term of office.

After 40 years of nonstop frenetic effort at reform with nothing (except in a few localities like Florida) to show for it, it's time to stop and rethink. We've spent most of our time for the last four decades working to obtain, implement, and sustain a series of incremental reforms. How many of those turned out to be worth the effort?

The problem is not that this or that incremental reform turned out not to be cost-effective. Incremental reform itself is turning out not to be cost-effective.

The Real Problem with the School Monopoly

I'm not counseling despair. We shouldn't give up—far from it! Indeed, if we start following the right strategy, there will be every reason for us to redouble our efforts.

But that assumes we do start following the right strategy. We desperately need to stop and rethink our approach. Education reform will only succeed if we invest in strategies that are cost-effective. For the last 40 years, in general and on the whole, education reformers have invested in strategies that weren't.

I'm not saying we haven't accomplished anything. There have been substantial victories that have produced real improvement in particular places.

Beyond all comparison, the most important of these have been the school voucher programs. Although vouchers improve education for those who use them, much more important is that vouchers are far and away the best-proven approach to reforming *public* schools. Eighteen high-quality empirical studies conducted in Milwaukee, Florida, Ohio, Texas, Maine, and Vermont have found that vouchers improve public schools. Not one study ever found that they harm public schools.[5] No other education reform has generated anything like that kind of evidence of success.

But nationwide, taking all things together, the education system hasn't budged in spite of Herculean efforts to reform it. The NAEP data show that clearly.

Ultimately, the only way to make school reform work is to break the government monopoly. Superficially, the landscape appears to be complex: we face an interweaving of multiple threats to reform and innovation. But the monopoly is the one decisive factor that reinforces all the other problems and keeps political power flowing to the hands of the worst, most destructive agents. The blob isn't just a powerful enemy of reform; it's the thing that makes all enemies of reform powerful. (Ask Mayor Fenty.) Our other problems won't instantly disappear if we break the monopoly, but they will become manageable.

It isn't simply that the monopoly renders meaningful school accountability impossible by ensuring that schools are never held responsible for their failure to perform. That alone is certainly a huge obstacle, of course; where the system answers to itself rather than to the people it's supposed to serve, failure creates no consequences.

Not every school will fail so much that it becomes "a failure" overall, but whatever failures actually occur—and in every school you can bet that *something* is failing—that failure will survive all efforts to wipe it out.

And it isn't simply that the monopoly, by its very nature, gives a tight-knit cluster of institutions—unions, education schools, and so forth—uncontested and unaccountable control of large amounts of money and power. Although that, too, is a huge obstacle by itself. Any serious concentration of power without accountability is always a recipe for corruption and exploitation, because the first thing such concentrated power gets used for is defending the concentration of power itself.

The unions' ability to spend millions on politics annually and turn out large numbers of self-interested voters and volunteers to protect the blob's gravy train are only the most obvious ways in which the monopoly empowers its own political protectors. Other aspects of this problem are less obvious but even more insidious. For many state legislators, the government school system is their district's primary employer and purchaser of goods. And education schools, which are unbreakably tied to the blob through teacher licensure requirements, are in turn a cash cow for the universities—ensuring that the universities (with only a few exceptions) are, and will remain, the blob's obedient servants.

Bad as these aspects of the problem are, they do not reach the deepest extent of the challenge. The monopoly is the key obstacle to school reform not primarily because it facilitates dysfunction but because it preempts innovation.

I once heard Milton Friedman remark that in all of society education is the only thing we still do more or less the same way we did it a hundred years ago. This is a profound reflection on just how deeply the monopoly destroys the system.

The unspeakable inner-city schools where kids are warehoused like stock animals rather than given the opportunity to learn are more shocking to our sensibilities, and in one sense rightly so. The pure shamelessness of the system in perpetuating these atrocities year after year, and of the unions and the rest of the blob in defending the system, is an outrage unique in kind.

But if we set aside the flagrancy of the offense and think solely in terms of pure magnitude of educational malpractice, perhaps we ought to be even more shocked by the fact that *in our very best schools*, students are still being educated in roughly the same way their great-grandparents were educated.

By comparison, consider the difference between 1911 medicine and 2011 medicine. Male life expectancy at birth in 1910 was 45 in New York and 46 in Boston. A human life in 1911 offered only half as much as it does now—and the half that it offered included unspeakably more physical suffering due to illness and injury than most of us know in our relatively pain-free lives. Why the change? Innovation.

(Even those 1910 figures were a dramatic improvement created by innovation. In 1880 the figures were only 29 and 37, respectively.)[6]

Or compare transportation. In 1911 the Model T had only been in production for three years, and the Wright Company had just offered the first airplane available for sale the previous year. It had only been eight years since Wilbur and Orville had successfully flown all of 200 feet at Kitty Hawk, taking the Wright Flyer I up to the dizzying altitude of ten whole feet.[7] Needless to say, humanity was at that time radically limited by the constraints of locality. Today, the world is our oyster. Why? Innovation.

Or hold up 1911 and 2011 and compare them on almost any other dimension. Communication? In 1911 radios got one station, movie projectors were hand-cranked—with no sound—and the first coast-to-coast phone call was still four years away. Food? Upton Sinclair's exposé of horrible sanitation in the meatpacking industry, *The Jungle*, came out in 1906. Domestic drudgery? Consider what it would have been like to keep your house and everything in it clean—from clothes and dishes to the baby's (nondisposable) diapers—with almost nothing but soap, water and elbow grease.

The list goes on and on; every aspect of our lives has been transformed, radically for the better, by innovation. Except education.

Why? Monopoly preempts innovation.

The Hidden Costs, and the *Hidden* Hidden Costs, of Monopoly

We often glide past this point without stopping to carefully consider its full meaning. It is important to have a well-rounded understanding of why monopoly preempts innovation. Most of the ways in which this happens are not just hidden from ordinary view, they're hidden even from the people who think they see the "hidden" costs.

School choice advocates have a tendency to focus exclusively on the absence of penalties for failure in the monopoly system. Certainly, the absence of penalties for failure is a titanic obstacle to improvement and a great friend and comforter to every enemy of real reform.

But even more important than the absence of penalties for failure is the absence of rewards, and especially the absence of certain kinds of rewards, for success. And even more important than that is the fact that "failure" and "success" are defined without reference to the only criterion that ultimately matters—parent satisfaction. And even more important than *that* are the barriers to entry for starting new schools and new school systems.

The Satisfaction of Success

Whenever anyone discusses the role of incentives in education, there is a certain kind of person who stands up and announces huffily, "teachers don't go into teaching to get paid!" The standard answer from the reformers is that nonmaterial incentives certainly do play a role in shaping teachers' and schools' behavior, but material incentives also play a role, and a powerful one. If the material incentives are wrong, they undermine the system regardless of how well aligned the nonmaterial incentives are.

I think that's true as far as it goes. But I think there's something else we should say that's even more important.

Of course teachers don't go into teaching to get paid—almost nobody goes into any job simply to get paid. Even the slacker who hates all work and just wants to make a few bucks to pay the rent needs to choose from among several competing job options, and I doubt if the paycheck is ever the only factor in that decision. And certainly when we're looking at professional white-collar workers, we can say with confidence that virtually none of them is selecting what profession to go into by comparing the size of paychecks.

People choose their professions because they want to accomplish something. Doctors want to heal. Engineers want to build.

Lawyers—even down to the scummiest of the jackpot-verdict shysters—want to see justice done. And teachers want to teach.

Economists tend to undervalue the role of incentives associated with intangible things. But it's clear enough to anyone who will stop and think about it that the satisfaction associated with accomplishing important things is a much more important economic motivator than mere pay. And if you want systematic empirical evidence to back that up, it's there to be found.[8]

It takes two big things to sustain that kind of motivation. First, people need to know whether they're succeeding or failing at their core task. Second, the people who succeed need to be rewarded—not with money and other material motives, but with meaningful recognition for accomplishment, advancement, and (above all) more freedom to take on larger tasks and do things in new ways, in order to accomplish even bigger and better things.

In particular, in every profession it's the innovators—the people who always want to take on bigger jobs and attack problems in new ways—who are most motivated by the desire for accomplishment. The popular image that associates the entrepreneurial mindset with greed is a pure myth. It's the time-servers and slackers who are more sensitive to directly material motives like paychecks and hours worked. Not coincidentally, in every profession the people who actually do accomplish the really big and really important things are the innovators.

This brings us to the first of the hidden ways in which the monopoly destroys innovation. The education monopoly is actually designed to drive anyone whose primary motive is to accomplish things out of the teaching profession, and to attract time-servers and slackers.

You want to measure your performance and find out whether you're doing a good job of teaching? Out come the long knives. The visceral hatred with which the official representatives of the teaching profession react to any suggestion of measuring performance—whether by tests or by parental satisfaction—shows that they recognize how their system is essentially built around the denial of recognition for success.

And God help you if you want to strike out in new directions and actually do great things. It doesn't matter whether you try to do it within the monopoly system, through a program like Teach for America, or outside it in private schools, or sort of halfway in and halfway out in charter schools. The bitter jealousy of the status quo will level every engine of dishonesty and treachery toward your destruction.

But if you want to be rewarded for jumping through hoops and serving time, welcome to paradise! The more years you serve, the more you'll be paid, regardless of whether you do anything worthwhile or not. And you can bump up the size of your paycheck by getting meaningless pieces of paper (teaching certificates, degrees in education) that are consistently shown to have no measurable impact on teaching.[9]

Not all teachers conform to this model, of course. But it is simply a fact that teachers who do conform to this model are rewarded with what they want (pay and tenure) while those who refuse to conform to it are punished with a never-ending river of vicious opprobrium. That can't help but have an impact on who goes into the profession and who doesn't.

If you don't believe me, listen to America's teachers. Public Agenda surveyed 900 teachers—a very serious survey size—and found that their attitudes about teaching fell into three distinct categories. At 40 percent of all teachers, the largest category is the one Public Agenda labels "disheartened." These teachers complain that they can't teach effectively, blaming various administrative and systematic obstacles. They're no longer interested in fighting for change; they're just lumping along bitterly toward retirement. Another 37 percent of teachers are "contented." They like their pay, hours, and working conditions. Unlike the disheartened, they've made a comfortable niche for themselves in the system; but, like the disheartened, they aren't really interested in change. Only 23 percent, the "idealists," conform to the image that most parents have of a good teacher—they believe all children can learn, and they're determined to do what it takes to teach their children effectively in spite of the lousy system.[10]

My coauthor Christian D'Andrea and I confirmed the connection to the monopoly last year in a study of federally collected survey data from over 52,000 teachers. Public school teachers have lower job satisfaction, less autonomy, and less influence in their schools than private school teachers. They aren't as empowered to keep order, their administrators and peers are not as supportive, and they're less safe. Just about the only thing they have more of is burnout.[11]

Less than a quarter of the teaching profession have the attitudes about teaching that we want in our teachers. That is the government school monopoly's real legacy. As long as the government school monopoly lasts, education won't change, because teachers won't change.

The Definition of Success

But what counts as "success" in the first place? We always think we know this better than we really do. Back in the 1970s, Detroit used to think it was highly successful because the big, unreliable, inefficient cars it was making sold in good numbers. Then Honda and Toyota came in and showed them just how unsuccessful they actually were.

In the business world there has been a complete revolution in thinking over the last generation about what counts as success. Management theorists like Peter Drucker have taught business leaders that *the only standard of organizational success that matters is customer satisfaction.*

Organizations have a natural tendency to define success without reference to the judgment of some outside client or customer—the person who actually uses the product or benefits from the service. That's because they don't like to be held accountable—judged—by people outside their organization! Much better to hold *yourself* accountable—accountable to some standard that you define and measure for yourself. When this happens, the organization becomes self-serving because it is detached from any standard of success other than its own judgment of itself.

But customer satisfaction doesn't just provide an external standard that facilitates accountability. It provides the right external standard. What do these organizations exist for, if they don't benefit people? If GM makes cars that don't satisfy drivers, what is GM for?

People generally resist this kind of thinking, I believe, because they fear subjectivity. We've been taught that empirical science is the ultimate paradigm of certainty and legitimacy. So we're perpetually searching for some empirical measurement of "real" success that won't involve anybody exercising his or her own judgment. The size of the engine, the horsepower, the fuel efficiency, the safety rating—anything other than whether or not the people who actually drive the car actually like it.

Closely related to this fear of subjectivity and obsession with objective metrics is the worship of expertise. Why should ordinary drivers be the ones to decide what counts as a good car? What do they know about the highly complex and technical process of manufacturing an automobile? Much better for me to select a panel of car experts and ask them whether the cars I make are any good—or better yet, just ask myself, since nobody is a bigger expert on my own carmaking than me.

Now, don't get me wrong. I'm a scientist myself, and I believe in the importance of objective facts, empirical knowledge, and expertise. You certainly can't make a car without them.

But the idea that we can use these things as our ultimate standard of success is wrong. And it's based on a colossal swindle—namely the idea, never stated but always implicit, that nobody's personal judgment is involved in selecting the metrics in the first place.

Both what the experts choose to measure as "success" and how they choose to measure it involve people using their judgment. If those metrics become the only permissible standard of success, then the organization won't serve the people it's supposed to serve; it will serve the experts—and usually a set of experts that it chooses for itself.

In the business world, the dysfunctions created when you aren't serving your customers quickly become clear. People buy less of your product and start looking for alternatives. Before long, more entrepreneurial organizations come in and eat your lunch, and if you don't wake up really quickly and start serving your customers, the entrepreneurs finish your lunch and get to work on your dinner.

But when there's a monopoly, this whole dynamic is concealed. And that goes double when there's a monopoly on an essential service everybody needs. Nobody is going to stop going out and obtaining education services. The monopoly makes it very difficult—much more expensive than it should be—to obtain services from alternative providers.

So the system defines success as whatever the system wants it to be, and everybody accepts this as the legitimate definition. From time to time the expert class will get into a fight over which expert-approved definition of success is preferable. But the expert class's monopoly on the right to judge what counts as success is unchallenged.

The only reason schools exist is to serve parents by helping them educate their children. But parent satisfaction—the only external reference available given that the system is government owned, and the only standard that measures whether schools are doing what is actually their job—is almost completely discredited as a legitimate measurement of school success.

I think it's incredibly important that schools teach kids basic reading and math skills. But I also think it's incredibly important that schools teach kids the basics of moral character—honesty, courage, responsibility, and so on. And it's incredibly important to teach every child an entrepreneurial mindset—the value of diligent service to others, productive innovation, and prudent risk taking. How do we measure those traits? I believe they probably are measurable, but there is no social consensus on the right way to measure them. Should the government anoint a set of experts to do it? Or what if the government disagrees with my assessment that these are important aspects of education?

If the system (or its anointed experts) decides for itself what children learn regardless of whether parents agree, it's basically set up in advance to sabotage anything schools do *except* what is self-serving and dysfunctional. Not only that, but my freedom—and my children's!—has been compromised. Everyone sees this when it comes to the politically sensitive issue of teaching children moral character, which is why government schools have stopped teaching moral character. But the same point applies across the board.

The Opportunity for Success

But the most important thing above all is to remove the barriers to creating new schools and new school systems. I'm amazed at how few people in the school choice movement grasp this point. If you take nothing else away from this chapter, take this: the primary goal of school choice programs should be to facilitate the emergence of new schools.

And I don't mean the creation of new schools within existing private school systems. Current school choice programs, laboring under the weight of ridiculous restrictions on their operation, don't facilitate the creation of truly new—innovative and entrepreneurial—schools; they just transfer students from the government school system to existing private school systems. The existing private school systems have no trouble expanding capacity to take the new entrants; there is really no such thing as fixed "capacity" in a school. As necessary, they even build new school buildings. But it takes more than a new building to truly make a new school. Few genuinely new schools—schools that aren't just extensions of existing school systems—are created.

This just perpetuates the status quo, with the marginal improvement that some students are transferred from the government's execrable system to a somewhat (but not radically) better system. We're moving kids from the government's 1911 schools to the equivalent of, say, 1917 schools. We'll never get 2011 schools that way.

Existing private schools are not going to cut it. They're better than public schools, but not by nearly as much as they should be.

The government system is so huge that it dominates the education sector. Teacher training, for example, is a wholly owned subsidiary of the blob. And fully one-third of private school teachers have previously taught in public schools.[12]

These days, people are starting to realize how destructive the current structure of the teaching profession in public schools is. Private schools are not formally bound to this structure; without union contracts, they have some room to maneuver. But the teacher workforce from which they draw their employees is still essentially a union workforce, with all the dysfunctions that implies.

However, more important than the blob's institutional dominance is its cultural dominance. The government school system dominates the culture, forming our idea of what counts as a "good school." Few private schools even have the idea that it might be possible to challenge this reigning orthodoxy. The thought just doesn't occur to them. So most private schools don't even make much use of the limited ability to reform that they do have. They remain slavish imitations of the government system.

What hinders the creation of new schools is not primarily legal and regulatory barriers. In many states such barriers are high, but they're not the most important problem. And legal and regulatory barriers are actually surprisingly low in some states.[13] If that kind of barrier were the problem, we could just set up school choice in one of the low-barrier states.

In fact, we already have. Florida, the nation's leading school choice state, also has the nation's lowest legal and regulatory barriers to creating private schools.[14] If that kind of barrier were the problem, Florida's school choice programs would be the solution. But they're not—not in their current form, anyway.

The real problem is that government schools give away education services for free. (Free at the point of service, anyway—ask taxpayers whether they're really free. We all learned long ago that there's no such thing as a free lunch!) That's why it's correct to call the government school system a monopoly even though there are private schools. In economics and in U.S. law, "monopoly" doesn't only refer to a sole provider; it also refers to an overwhelmingly predominant provider that can use its dominance to prevent other providers from effectively challenging its position.

Because the government gives away education services for free, there's very little customer base left for other providers. All schools other than government schools are being made to start the race 500 yards behind the starting line. With their legs tied together. And a butcher knife plunged through their backs.

I once heard Friedman make this point by asking his audience to imagine what would happen if the government gave away free hot dogs on every street corner. Most of the private hot dog vendors, he observed, would go out of business. Government would have a monopoly on hot dogs without having formally banned private hot dog providers. This, he said, is just what has happened in education.

This example could actually be expanded in an important way. Suppose, because of the First Amendment, the government's free hot dog stands were forbidden to sell kosher hot dogs. And let's say they didn't find it worthwhile to stock special hot dogs for people with allergies to specific ingredients or other specialized medical and dietary needs. And some high-end consumers were willing to pay a high price to continue getting hot dogs from more prestigious providers. If that were the case, private hot dog providers could survive by serving these niche markets.

That's exactly what the education sector looks like today. Existing private schools are merely the rump left behind by the destruction of the education market by the government monopoly. They survive by catering to niche markets that strongly desire specific services that they can't get from government schools—primarily religious instruction and a morally sound school culture, specialization in dealing with specific disabilities, or snobbish social prestige.

By giving parents rather than government schools control over where government education funding gets spent, universal school choice would mitigate the advantage of the government school system. Without the unfair cost advantage for public schools, many parents would choose private schools. This would allow the introduction of real alternative schools that could challenge the dominance of the government system.

Government schools would still have major advantages. They would still be widely thought of as the "default" school system. They would have access to much larger cash reserves to fund publicity campaigns. And although the schools themselves would no doubt keep their hands clean, their teacher and staff unions could be expected to dramatically expand their long-standing smear campaign against private schools, promoting an endless stream of lies and calumny in order to demonize any alternative to the public system.

Nevertheless, the innovative new private schools that could be created under such a system would have one huge advantage government schools wouldn't have. They'd be creating the 2011 school, while the government would still be offering the same old 1911 schools it has now.

Only Universal Choice Will Do the Job

So why don't school choice programs do this now? That's the question the school choice movement should be asking. Until we get this right, nothing else will really matter.

Rock-solid empirical research consistently finds that vouchers improve public schools. And no wonder, since parents will happily take a 1917 school over a 1911 school if you give them the option. So if they want to keep their students, those 1911-style public schools have to get it in gear and work their way up to the 1917 level that existing private schools are operating on. Yet even where there are school choice programs, we haven't seen much emergence of new models of schooling—2011 schools—in the private sector. What gives?

Existing school choice programs don't provide a large enough, strong enough or free enough customer base to build new schools on. They're not allowed to; the limits and restrictions that are built into all existing school choice programs don't permit them to.[15]

This compromise is the price we started paying 20 years ago to get programs enacted, and we have kept paying it ever since. The compromise was probably wise at the time—universal school choice wasn't likely to happen in 1990. But we do need to acknowledge that we have never grown our way out of that compromise, as we had hoped we would. And we need to take account of what we have lost as a result.

Existing programs don't provide a customer base that is large enough. The voucher programs are only allowed to serve narrow populations like the poor or the disabled. As Friedman always used to say, show me a program that's limited to the poor and I'll show you a poor program.

The tax-credit programs are limited to a fixed number of total dollars, meaning a fixed number of students. You could never get school choice for every child on that model, and without school choice for every child we can't break the monopoly. (Even if existing fixed-dollar limits on tax-credit programs were removed, narrow limitations on their size would still be inherent in their structure; people only pay a certain amount in state taxes. Refundable credits would do it, but tax-credit advocates aren't seeking that, and legislators will never vote to create billions of dollars' worth of refundable credits anyway.)

In both cases, the total population the programs are allowed to serve is a small portion of the population. School choice needs to serve all students before educational innovators will have a customer base that gives them space to create.

Existing programs don't provide a customer base that is strong enough in its ability to purchase education services. Only a portion, usually a small portion, of the funding public schools get is available to students exercising school choice. A small voucher buys a small amount of choice. Educational innovators won't need as much money as the unbelievably bloated government system spends, but they have to have *something* to work with.

This limitation is especially problematic for tax-credit programs. Educational tax credits or deductions on people's personal taxes are currently limited to tiny amounts, and even if they weren't, people only pay so much in taxes. Scholarship programs funded through tax credits for contributions don't fare much better. Given that they operate—and must always operate—under dollar-value ceilings, they typically try to spread the money around to help as many students as possible. As a result, average scholarship values in these programs range between about $1,000 and $2,000.[16]

And existing programs don't provide a customer base that is free enough. This is the area where the problems with existing programs are least serious, but it still deserves mention. School choice programs restrict what participating schools are allowed to do—required administration of state tests is a growing problem, since it effectively pressures schools to conform to the government-approved curriculum.

And they are sometimes designed to be unfriendly to new schools, requiring them to clear high hurdles in order to demonstrate that they aren't fly-by-night operators. These provisions are often included less to satisfy wavering legislators and more to keep the big private school systems in the school choice coalition. The big, old-guard private school systems don't want to allow innovators a chance to take their business any more than the government monopoly does.

The school choice movement desperately needs to change its conceptual framework. We think too much in terms of providing an alternative to, or (at best) fixing, the dysfunctions of public schools. Our model should not be "fix the dysfunctions" but "empower innovation." We need to stop offering school choice as a way to transfer students from 1911 schools into 1917 schools, or even to transform the 1911 schools themselves into 1917 schools. We need to start offering it as a way to build 2011 schools.

That means we need to renew our goal of enacting not just school choice, but universal school choice. Universal choice is not just a way to build 2011 schools. It's the only way to build them.

In the short run, there are a lot of small things we can do to make things incrementally better. Not just marginal choice programs but also other reforms—alternative teacher training, tenure reform, and so forth. But it takes incredible sacrifice just to create one of those programs. If short-run benefits are the only benefits we're going to get out of them, they're not worth the price.

And if it's the long run we're interested in, none of those reforms will endure as long as the power of the monopoly gives the blob all the power it needs to capture or undermine them. And destroying the monopoly—which is another way of saying "enacting universal choice"—wouldn't just create radical improvement in schools by itself; it would also make all those other ways of improving schools sustainable.

We can either break the school monopoly or be broken by it.

But Can It Happen?

If I'm right, it follows that we all ought to quit bothering with education reform and go do something more productive with our lives— unless universal choice can actually happen. But can it?

I think it not only can, but it likely will. However, in the past our movement has succumbed to the temptations of overconfidence. So let me begin with a note of caution.

The Long Road to Victory

Friedman was a brilliant economist, but as a political analyst he had his limitations. Throughout his life, his high expectations for the political success of vouchers were disappointed time and time again. His economist's mind saw clearly that a universal voucher program was just obviously the right policy. Everybody would win, except for the leeches who make their living by destroying children's lives. Propaganda and lies might obscure the truth for a time. But vouchers were so right, how could people fail to see the truth before long? And seeing it, how could they fail to do the right thing?

Even up through the last years of his life, he predicted he would live to see the enactment of universal vouchers in at least one state—a bold prediction for a man who had seen the far side of 90 and was making jokes about having "outlived the actuarial tables." He died in 2006 at age 94, undaunted and steadfast to the end in his defense of educational freedom, yet without having lived to see the victory.

He believed so much in the power of good ideas that he never gave sufficient weight to the power of bad ideas. Vouchers really are the obviously right policy—they really do benefit everyone except the leeches. But the leeches have spent the last century (since at least Dewey) taking control of our culture and shaping our whole worldview. They haven't just mowed down the flowers of liberty; they've sown salt in the soil. That was never going to be undone in a day.

Our problem is that we focus too much on this or that particular political battle and not on the long, slow culture war between those who are loyal to freedom and those who—out of ignorance or malice—serve collectivism. Whether we win this year's version of the Battle of Inchon or the Tet Offensive is important. But what really matters is the great overarching Cold War, which was a contest not between two armies but between two ways of life, spanning decades and ultimately decided by which civilization had the shared determination to outlast the other.

In fact, the Cold War provides a useful analogy. On paper, the Soviets had all the worldly advantages. They had more men, they had more tanks, they had more of everything you can count. And let's face it: they had more guts. They were ruthless, always playing to win; too often we fought them with one hand tied behind our backs.

When you boil it down to essentials, we only had two really big advantages in the Cold War. We had the entrepreneurial spirit—a culture that was relentlessly hungry for constructive innovation, productive achievement, and diligence in the service of authentic human needs. And we had the incalculable advantage of a just cause—we were right and they were wrong, and deep in their hearts, both sides knew it.

And guess what? It turns out those are the only advantages you ultimately need.

Like the Red Army, Bull Connor had all the guns, all the dogs, all the hoses, all the money, and all the power. What did Martin Luther King have?

When you're playing for the really big stakes, the once-in-a-lifetime changes in fundamental social institutions, bet on a just cause and an entrepreneurial spirit before any amount of worldly power.

Just be prepared to be patient.

The Danger of Losing Hope and Lowering Our Standards

The Cold War even speaks to where we are in the present moment. While the idea of vouchers is centuries old, the modern school choice movement dates to the creation of the Milwaukee voucher program in 1990. We're about 20 years into this fight. If we date the start of the Cold War to the years after World War II and count about 20 years forward, that puts us right in the thick of Vietnam.

The reason we lost in Vietnam, and then went on to endure a decade of humiliation after humiliation at the hands of the Soviets, was because we temporarily gave up our two great advantages. Too many Americans traded in the entrepreneurial spirit for a materialistic selfishness that found satisfaction in comfort and security rather than innovation and achievement. And above all, too many of us lost our faith in freedom, in the rightness of our cause. Who were we to say that our way was better than the Soviet way?

Right now I fear the school choice movement could be about to make the same disastrous mistake. Some of the people who used to be stalwart champions of real choice are now giving voice to a palpable sense of pessimism about vouchers.[17] Even after 20 whole years, the blob has not yet dropped at our feet and sued for peace, offering us everything we wish. Obviously we need to look elsewhere for meaningful reform; vouchers don't work, or they don't work unless we go fix a lot of other problems first.

The underlying problem here is the increasing tendency among these wavering figures to pooh-pooh the real achievements vouchers have delivered so far. One discouraged voucher supporter, for example, erroneously laments that "there is little evidence that voucher or choice programs have succeeded in fostering the emergence or expansion of high-quality options."[18] In fact, as has been noted above, all the empirical evidence consistently says otherwise.

It's one thing to acknowledge this evidence and then argue that these accomplishments aren't good enough. That would be well worth applauding. (In fact, I think it would be such a good thing that I'm doing it right now in this chapter!) But to talk as though vouchers have accomplished little or nothing is a disservice.

To see why it matters so much, look again at the Cold War analogy. In the 1950s and 1960s, intellectual elites started pooh-poohing America's past accomplishments. They wanted to smash complacency and call the rising generation of Americans to be better, reach for a higher vision—to reboot America with even more lofty expectations.

What they got instead was hippies who had no interest in contributing to society, much less building a better and greater one. The elites who pooh-poohed America's past didn't produce a new generation eager to pursue a high vision, but a new generation that pursued visions by getting high. Nothing symbolizes this more than draft dodging. Why fight for America against the communist threat—what has America done to deserve it?

Now we have people who should know better pooh-poohing the real accomplishments of vouchers. It's hard to doubt that if this narrative sets in, the next thing we're going to see is a bunch of education reform hippies committing a similar dereliction of duty, refusing to serve in the only army that can save their country from the blob.

In Vietnam and afterward, the loss of faith that freedom *should* win in the end was intimately connected with a loss of faith that freedom *would* win in the end. Communism might be bad, we were told, but it's here to stay. Efforts to destroy it have accomplished nothing. We need to start treating the Soviets with respect and find a modus vivendi, a compromise that ensures coexistence. That way we have some chance to do some good, maybe be a force for reform within the Soviet system.

That kind of thinking took us right off the rails in the 1970s. As long as we accepted Soviet tyranny as an eternal fact of life, we were repeatedly stymied, humiliated, and demoralized. Only when we regained our courage and went back to thinking of it as an enemy to be defeated did we start winning battles again.

You know why? Compromise with an evil system can be fine as a short-term tactical need; we have to live in the real world, not a utopia. But when compromise with the evil system becomes too important to us—when we lose our fundamental drive to defeat it and create something better—then there's no more mission. We have no real alternative to offer. People might as well just sign up with the oppressor. It pays better.

If we can overcome our political myopia and look past the limits of the one-year political cycle, the long-term cultural conditions for universal choice are better than ever and are only going to improve. The empirical data showing that existing voucher programs improve public schools points to the huge potential of universal choice. The unions have lost the war of ideas—they now have no credibility, even in the dinosaur media. The recent success of charter schools and the shifting of the balance of power within the political left have established parental choice in education as a bipartisan principle. And as people begin to realize the inherent limits of charters—which, being government owned and hobbled at one leg to the status quo, will never deliver the kind of radical innovation that's needed in education—over time vouchers will emerge as the only way to fulfill the promise of parental choice. A new generation is rising that takes for granted the value of expansive personal choice and understands the dysfunctions created by top-down control. And technological innovation in every other area of life is making it easier to see how educational entrepreneurship could transform learning in radically positive ways.

Remember, Martin Luther King wrote his most famous manifesto while sitting in Bull Connor's jail in Birmingham. Where would we be now if he had just written, "Well, here I am in jail, I guess I've failed"?

He knew that however bad things might look, however Connor might beat him in terms of visible "stuff," he had the invisible advantages: justice, courage, and entrepreneurial shrewdness. And that meant in the end, he would have Connor licked.

Given all our inherent advantages, we have every right to appropriate the same confidence. If we don't, then once again—shame on us.

The Hidden Victory of School Choice: All the Other Reforms

Shakespeare's plays are typically divided into three genres: comedy, tragedy, and history. There's a lesson there for the school choice movement. When people make up a story from whole cloth, they usually make it a story of triumph or a story of defeat. But the true stories—the histories—don't fall neatly into either of those models. They're a separate category.

Some people like to tell the story of the school choice movement as a success story. Others like to tell it as a story of defeat. The reality is more complicated.

The Life Cycle of School Choice

The story of school choice thus far is a cycle that has repeated itself several times. First, the movement compromises its ideal in order to get programs enacted. It works to create new school choice programs that aren't what the advocates really want—they're tiny in size, they're burdened with regulations—but they're the best the movement thinks it can get. We saw this for the first time in 1990, with the creation of the first modern voucher program in Milwaukee. The original program served only a tiny handful of students, who only had access to a tiny handful of schools.

Then, for a while, the movement has success. New programs get created. And there is palpable movement toward the ideal of universal choice; the mystique of the monopoly is chipped away, and public opinion becomes friendlier to offering more choice to more people. In Milwaukee, the program was expanded from hundreds of students to thousands, then tens of thousands.

But then comes the plateau. New programs continue to get enacted, but they stop moving the ball toward universal choice. Momentum toward the ideal stalls. School choice looks burned out. After Milwaukee, vouchers didn't expand much; Ohio enacted a program offering pitifully small-value vouchers to Cleveland students in 1995, but that was it.

And then the movement ratchets up its expectations and rallies for a new assault. The old programs aren't good enough anymore. The movement demands something better.

And it gets it. One or more breakthrough programs take choice to a new level, and then other programs follow suit. In 1998, the U.S. Supreme Court blessed the expansion of the Milwaukee program to include the vast majority of private schools, and this raised expectations for school choice reformers nationwide.

There was a burst of new school choice programs, and they made substantial progress toward universal choice compared to Milwaukee. Arizona created a tax-credit scholarship program with no income restrictions in 1998. Florida created the McKay program for disabled students, again with no income restrictions, in 1999; it also created a failing-schools voucher in that year, and shortly thereafter a (low-income) tax-credit scholarship program. Pennsylvania created a tax-credit scholarship (with an income restriction, but a moderate one compared with Milwaukee's) in 2001. Illinois and Minnesota created new personal tax-credit and deduction programs for parents paying private school tuition.

And then, another plateau. The movement stalled again. The only programs created in the next few years were a program for autistic students (a tiny student population) in Ohio in 2003, and the DC voucher program in 2004—which was intentionally designed to insulate public schools from the effects of competition from vouchers.

But after a time, the movement regrouped again and renewed its assault again, once more ratcheting up expectations to a new level. And this time, it didn't get a burst of new programs but an explosion. In 2005, Ohio enacted an ambitious failing-schools voucher reaching every major city in the state, and Utah adopted a program on Florida's McKay model. In 2006, tax-credit scholarship programs were created in Arizona, Iowa, and Rhode Island. Arizona also enacted two small voucher programs serving disabled and foster children. And in the same two years, existing school choice programs were expanded nationwide—dollar caps were raised, eligibility was expanded, and new schools were permitted to participate.

It was a heady time to be a school choice advocate, as I can testify from experience. The wind was at our backs.

And then we lost that momentum. As of 2007, another plateau was upon us.

One reason for this was that vouchers suffered a single defeat—but a very high-profile one. Utah enacted a voucher with universal eligibility; the dollar values were on a sliding scale and most residents would have gotten low dollar values, but it would have been a major move toward the goal. Unfortunately, an obscure provision of Utah law allowed the unions to overturn the new program by referendum in a special election. The unions never have any problem getting thousands of self-interested voters to show up at the polls even when there's nothing else on the ballot, while regular voters don't generally go to the polls except for regular elections, so the result was foreordained.

Utah was not the only reason the national momentum for vouchers dispersed. We'll look at another important reason in just a moment. But it would be foolish to say Utah played no role. However it came to pass, another plateau followed.

The current plateau has had more activity than the previous ones. Georgia adopted another McKay-style voucher in 2007 and a tax-credit scholarship the following year. Louisiana adopted two extremely small—hardly worth mentioning, really—programs in 2008. Indiana adopted a tax-credit scholarship in 2009; Oklahoma adopted a McKay-style voucher in 2010.

Yet for all that, it is still a plateau—because we're not moving the ball toward universal choice. The programs enacted in 2009 and 2010 aren't substantially closer to universal choice than the programs enacted during the big 2005–2006 rally.

Surveying this whole history, we can see that the trajectory has been uneven, but overall it has been in the right direction. We may not be traveling on a straight, easy upward line. But neither are we going in circles. It's a spiral—around and around, but heading upward over time.

What we need in 2011 is not a new trajectory. It's a new rally for a new assault—with a new ratcheting up of expectations to move us up the spiral toward universal choice.

Introducing Standards, Testing, Charters,
Tenure Reform—Brought to You by Vouchers

This history helps us see that the voucher movement has delivered a lot more victories than it may at first appear. It has delivered them to other reform movements! Vouchers have made it politically possible to enact almost all the other major reforms we've tried in the past 20 years.

The blob knows that large-scale school choice is a mortal threat to its tyrannical dominance. It also knows that no other reform out there is such a threat. Thus, any time there's a threat to create widely available school choice, it will divert all its energy away from fighting other reforms and toward fighting choice.

Today's school choice programs are narrowly limited and burdened, but they have one form of power that can't be contained by those limits. They are a manifestation of the movement toward vouchers for all.

That's why the unions are so deeply, deeply invested in the line that small, narrow, constricted voucher programs are "the camel's nose under the tent" for universal vouchers. They're not afraid vouchers will fail, but they're terrified that vouchers will succeed! (You would think they'd realize how this line dramatically reveals their selfishness. But nobody ever said self-awareness was a particular strength of the unions' spokespeople.)

The hot, successful education reform of the late 1990s and early 2000s was standards and testing. The No Child Left Behind law was that movement's crowning achievement. And how did the reformers get it? By threatening to enact a national school choice program and then trading that away in exchange for votes in favor of standards and testing.

The hot, successful education reform of the mid to late 2000s was charter schools. By fall 2009 there were over 5,000 charter schools serving 1.5 million children.[19] How did the reformers get that? The unions were busy fighting off the explosion of voucher bills in state legislatures during the two great voucher surges in 1998–2001 and 2005–2006. Legislators, opinion leaders, and key institutions triangulated between vouchers and charters, using their opposition to vouchers as an excuse to support charters. As long as vouchers were a real threat, they could tell their union allies to suck it up and accept that they'd be supporting charters. The alternative would be someone who supports both charters and vouchers.

Even the unions themselves sometimes had to pretend to like charters! Why do you think they'd do that? So that they could viciously oppose vouchers while showing that they weren't against all reform.

This is the other major reason—more important, I think, than the Utah defeat—for the end of the 2005–2006 voucher rally. Charters used the voucher rally to launch a dramatic series of successes, and the success of charters drew off the political capital in the reform movement.

These days the hot, new policy is tenure reform. And if you listen carefully, you'll hear the people supporting tenure reform triangulating against vouchers to a large extent, just like the accountability and charter people did.

Tenure reform is still in the early stages. It sounds really exciting, primarily because few people have really tried to implement it yet. A handful of heroic reformers have had some local successes, but Rhee's fate illustrates how fragile those successes can be. I predict that however many opinion leaders may talk it up, tenure reform won't become a national policy wave until we see another major rally by the voucher movement. Then you'll *really* see tenure reform go big.

The reason vouchers haven't had more success is because every time they reach the part of their life cycle where they start winning, other reform movements swoop in and siphon off political capital by using this triangulation dynamic. They don't necessarily do it on purpose; this is just the way the political landscape is constructed. The more of a threat vouchers are, the more success other reforms will have. And that success, in turn, cools off the momentum for vouchers until the next stage of their life cycle.

And there's another kind of hidden victory vouchers have achieved. I mentioned above that the unions have lost the war of ideas. Even the dinosaur media—*Time, Newsweek,* the *Washington Post*—have gotten wise to the blob and its various intellectual swindles. That's one of the major reasons I'm bullish on the prospects for vouchers in the coming decade. Rhee on the cover of *Time* is like the election of Margaret Thatcher or the development of the Alberta oil sands; it shifts the whole strategic landscape our way.

And it was mostly our doing. We're the ones who developed the intellectual framework for understanding the government school system as a unionized, self-interested, exploitative monopoly rather than as an organic expression of America's democratic community life. Nobody talks about government schooling as "a pillar of American democracy" anymore. We did that.

This is why my thesis that only universal choice makes school reform worth fighting for can be reconciled with the observation that union power is declining. You might say, "If the unions have lost the battle of ideas, why are you saying we have to break the monopoly with universal choice in order to sustain real reform in the long term?" The answer is that it's only because we've been fighting for universal choice, threatening their monopoly, that the unions began to decline in the first place.

We in the school choice movement have a choice, and it's imperative that we choose wisely. We can get all bitter and resentful that other people are "taking" the political success that's "rightly" ours. Or we can accept reality, quit worrying about who gets the credit and applause, and feel proud that we're accomplishing so much good in the world. We're demolishing the unions' cultural hegemony and helping enact many other useful reforms as we move steadily up the spiral toward ever-more and ever-better voucher programs. Let's embrace that. Envy is a deadly sin. (If it helps, remember that while all sin leads to misery in the end, envy is the only sin that starts there.)

Universal Choice or Bust!

If we choose envy, we'll go to war with our natural allies (other reformers) and we'll lose. But if we choose humility, we can help ourselves win by helping them win.

You see, this "voucher threat" triangulation effect only works if the threat remains credible over time. If vouchers become nothing but a bogeyman to scare squishy legislators, pretty soon the squishy legislators won't be scared any more. (Just because they're squishy doesn't mean they're dumb.) Vouchers need to rally and get successful, or there'll be no more threat to triangulate against.

And it's not enough just to enact new programs. We have to be making progress toward universal vouchers. In themselves, small and overregulated voucher programs can't break the monopoly. They're a threat because they point to the possibility of monopoly-breaking universal vouchers. So if it ever becomes a settled narrative that the school choice movement can't get to universal vouchers, the threat vanishes. We have to make progress, and be seen making progress, toward the universal goal. We can still make compromises to get new programs, but the compromises have to become better and better for us over time, and worse for the unions.

And do you see what follows? If we have to be constantly making progress toward universal choice, eventually we have to actually get to universal choice. Zeno's paradox notwithstanding, if we keep moving toward a destination we must eventually reach it.

And that day must not be infinitely delayed. As every economist knows, the human mind discounts the value of costs and benefits for the time delay before they're realized. In other words, the further off in the future universal vouchers are, the less weight people give them. We need to make progress, and be seen making progress, toward universal vouchers in the concrete, foreseeable future, not in some far-off paradise.

The Next Step: What?

How should we ratchet up expectations as we rally for a new assault? There might be many ways of putting that ambition into practice when it comes to the details. But here are two basic principles I would propose to guide our efforts.

We should start explicitly making universal choice the goal of our movement. We need to quit talking as if we're not out to revolutionize education. When opponents of new programs argue that "this will be the camel's nose under the tent for universal vouchers," we should say, "if the program works, then yes, we would be crazy not to expand it!"

We need to internalize and institutionalize the lesson that constant progress toward universal choice is the only thing that can make our movement powerful. The cycle of strong, ratcheted-up demands followed by compromises for the sake of enacting new programs has not always meant strong *universalist* rhetoric. That needs to change.

We can have different opinions about when and how much it's prudent to compromise. But the movement needs to send a clear signal that, whatever our internal divisions over matters of prudence, we are on the march to universal choice. The people who don't want to send that signal are not really in favor of vouchers at all; they're just using vouchers as a means of redistributing wealth. Let's clarify who's really fighting for what.

And we should focus our efforts on innovative proposals that move the ball further down the road toward universal choice but are still politically achievable. Personally, I think universal choice in a state would be possible in the next three years, if we really wanted it and focused our efforts on getting it. But if that's too much to ask, we can pick a less daring goal. One example might be creating truly universal choice in a medium- to large-sized metro area.

By "focus our efforts," I primarily mean we need to stop spending valuable time and resources promoting the creation of any new program that doesn't clearly advance us toward the goal of universal choice. Even if a program would be an improvement over the status quo, it's not worth the extraordinary effort it would take to create it unless it helps us win the long war. More limited programs, such as those enacted in the last decade in Washington DC, Rhode Island,

and Louisiana may have represented progress toward universal choice compared with where we were in, say, 1998. But they wouldn't represent progress if they were enacted today. We shouldn't bother creating new programs on that model any more. We can wish them well, but our resources are scarce and they should be focused where they can do the most good.

The Next Step: When?

How long must we wait for universal choice? I think this is the most urgent question facing the movement right now.

Above, I've counseled caution. To avoid despair, we need to keep our eyes on winning the long war. When you're mired in the depths of Vietnam, it's hard to look forward to the fall of the Berlin Wall. When you're sitting in Bull Connor's jail, it's hard to look forward to the signing of the Civil Rights Act. But that's what you have to do.

However, I've also spoken of the entrepreneurial spirit. If we lose that, we're dead. We shouldn't expect too much victory too fast. But when we stop demanding to see real victories in real time, we've lost the mission. Entrepreneurial people aren't satisfied to bunker down and hold territory. That'll kill our energy and spirit quicker than anything.

We're right to be impatient. And not just because it'll keep us fighting.

When the big victory does come, it's not likely to arrive gradually. Much of what we do between now and then will have to be gradual and incremental, but there's no reason to think that's how the last stages will go. Quite the contrary, history gives us every reason to think that the dam will break suddenly.

Consider the history of "monetarism," the economic theory for which Friedman is most famous in the world of professional economics. He promoted it for about 25 years before it was finally adopted at the national policy level by Ronald Reagan.

How does the story of those 25 years go? Small victory followed by small victory, piled up one upon the other until they reached the heights of national policy?

Just the opposite. As Friedman worked to develop his idea among a small network of highly potent intellectuals—the Chicago school—the policy world kept digging itself deeper and deeper into

Keynesianism. When Keynesian policies failed, they concluded that obviously what was needed was stronger doses of Keynesianism! Wage and price controls failed, and policymakers responded with tighter wage and price controls.

Any gambler will tell you what happens when you respond to failure by doubling down over and over again. Eventually, you crash. That's what happened, catastrophically, in the late 1970s.

Suddenly, the nation was ready for an alternative. And the Chicago school had one ready. Monetarism was radical, but the collapse of Keynesian planning was such a disaster that radicalism unexpectedly became a PR advantage. When the world is—or seems to be—falling apart, the incrementalists no longer sound prudent and wise but complacent and out of touch; the radicals no longer sound wild-eyed and irresponsible but brave and entrepreneurial. (It was the exact same dynamic, working in reverse, that brought Keynesianism roaring back in 2008.)

We can't predict the timeline for universal choice by extrapolating from our current rate of progress. It may take a long time. But it may happen soon.

The one thing we can—and must—do is seize opportunities whenever they're there to be seized. The time is ripe for a major new offensive that once again takes us to the next level up on the spiral. We need to break out dramatically from the mold of the 2000s and set a new, much higher bar for the 2010s that moves us visibly toward universal choice.

If we keep our courage, if we balance the fortitude of remembering that this is a long war with the entrepreneurial courage of playing offense and not defense, that spiral just may become a straight line a lot sooner than you think.

Notes

1. See, for example, Matt Ladner, "Checker Says RELAX!," http://jaypgreene .com/2010/07/29/checker-says-relax/, July 29, 2010 (accessed September 7, 2010).
2. Bobby Rampey, Gloria Dion, and Patricia Donahue, "The Nation's Report Card: Trends in Academic Progress in Reading and Mathematics 2008," Institute of Education Sciences, U.S. Department of Education, April 2009. Reading scores are first available for 1971, math scores for 1973. There has been some modest improvement in learning at earlier ages since NAEP

began, but that improvement is not being sustained through age 17 so it's not clear whether it counts for anything.

3. It would be a digression to go into a discussion of the excuses here; my coauthors and I have discussed them in Jay Greene, Greg Forster, and Marcus Winters, *Education Myths*, Rowman & Littlefield, Lanham, MD, 2005.

4. Digest of Education Statistics 2009, Institute of Education Sciences, U.S. Department of Education, April 2010, Table 103.

5. For the first 16 studies see Greg Forster, "A Win–Win Solution: The Empirical Evidence on How Vouchers Affect Public Schools," Foundation for Educational Choice, December 2008; the two more recent studies are Jay Greene and Ryan Marsh, "The Effect of Milwaukee's Parental Choice Program on Student Achievement in Milwaukee Public Schools," School Choice Demonstration Project, March 2009; and David Figlio and Cassandra Hart, "Competitive Effects of Means-Tested School Vouchers," revised April 2010. One additional study, in Washington, DC, found that vouchers had no visible impact on public schools; given that the DC voucher program is also the only program that is designed to intentionally insulate public schools from the impact of vouchers, this result is not surprising!

6. Edward Meeker, "The Social Rate of Return on Investment in Public Health, 1880–1910," *The Journal of Economic History*, 34 (1974): 392–421, p. 392.

7. "Inventing a Flying Machine," website of the National Air and Space Museum, http://www.nasm.si.edu/wrightbrothers/age/1910/index.cfm and http://www.nasm.si.edu/wrightbrothers/fly/1903/triumph.cfm (accessed May 6, 2010). The longest flight of the Wright Flyer I was actually 852 feet, but that flight ended in a crash that totaled the aircraft, so it might not qualify as a "successful" flight.

8. See Frederick Herzberg, "One More Time: How Do You Motivate Employees?" *Harvard Business Review*, original version published 1968; updated version published September/October 1987; republished January 2003. In the updated version, the editors of *Harvard Business Review* report that this article is the most requested among all articles it has ever published.

9. See Greene, Forster and Winters, *Education Myths*, chapter 5.

10. Jean Johnson, Andrew Yarrow, Jonathan Rochkind and Amber Ott, "Teaching for a Living: How Teachers See the Profession Today," Public Agenda, October 21, 2009.

11. Greg Forster and Christian D'Andrea, "Free to Teach: What America's Teachers Say about Teaching in Public and Private Schools," Foundation for Educational Choice, May 2009.

12. Forster and D'Andrea, "Free to Teach," p. 26.

13. Christopher Hammons, "Fifty Educational Markets: A Playbook of State Laws and Regulations Governing Private Schools," Foundation for Educational Choice, April 2008.

14. Hammons, "Fifty Educational Markets," p. 23. Florida is tied with New Jersey for the best score among the fifty states in Hammons' rating of burdensome regulations.

15. For more information on how each of the nation's existing school choice programs is restricted, see "School Choice Programs," Foundation for Educational Choice, http://www.edchoice.org/School-Choice/School -Choice-Programs.aspx (accessed September 7, 2010).

16. See "School Choice Programs," Foundation for Educational Choice, http://www.edchoice.org/School-Choice/School-Choice-Programs.aspx (accessed September 7, 2010). The only exceptions are Arizona's tiny program for disabled students (which began as a voucher program and was converted), Florida's program (where the scholarship amount is legislatively mandated at just below $4,000) and Rhode Island (which can afford to dole out almost $6,000 per student because it serves such a miniscule number of students—fewer than 300). Of these, only the Florida program is of any significant size; even that program is limited to low-income students and couldn't be scaled to the whole population.

17. See Frederick Hess, "After Milwaukee," The American, September 24, 2008 (Checker Finn is also quoted in this article).

18. Hess, "After Milwaukee."

19. See "Charter Connection," Center for Education Reform, http://www .edreform.com/Issues/Charter_Connection/?All_About_Charter _Schools (accessed September 28, 2010).

Contributors

George A. Clowes is a senior fellow for education policy at The Heartland Institute. He was the founding managing editor of Heartland's monthly newspaper, *School Reform News*, which began publication in January 1997 and has a current circulation of 24,700, including all state and national elected officials. During his eight-year editorial tenure, Clowes solicited and edited hundreds of articles reporting on the latest developments in school choice, school finance, curriculum, and other aspects of school reform. He also produced a lengthy interview each month with a leading figure in the school choice movement.

Andrew J. Coulson directs the Cato Institute's Center for Educational Freedom. He studies the relative merits of alternative school systems using historical and contemporary international evidence. His book *Market Education: The Unknown History* (Transaction, 1999) is the most comprehensive historical investigation of comparative school system organization. He is also the author of the most comprehensive review (for the *Journal of School Choice*) of the modern statistical literature comparing public, private, and truly free market school systems. His work has been published in peer-reviewed journals and in the pages of the *Wall Street Journal*, *Washington Post*, and many other newspapers.

Pauline Dixon is a senior lecturer in education and development at Newcastle University and is the director of research at the university's E.G. West Centre. Her work on private and government schools in slum and low income areas in Africa and Asia is extensive. She has published in scholarly peer reviewed journals including *School Effectiveness and School Improvement, Austrian Economic Review* and the *International Journal of Educational Research*.

Greg Forster is a senior fellow at the Foundation for Educational Choice, where he has conducted research and written about school choice policy. He has conducted empirical studies on the impact of school choice programs in Milwaukee, Cleveland, Florida, Ohio, and Texas, as well as national empirical studies of participation in school choice programs and the impact of charter schools. His research has appeared in the peer-reviewed publications *Teachers College Record* and *Education Working Paper Archive*, and his articles on education policy have appeared in the *Washington Post*, the *Los Angeles Times*, the *Philadelphia Inquirer*, *Education Next*, the *Chronicle of Higher Education*, and numerous other publications. He is the coauthor of *Education Myths: What Special-Interest Groups Want You to Believe about Our Schools—and Why It Isn't So* (Rowman & Littlefield, 2005).

Jay P. Greene is the endowed professor of education reform at the University of Arkansas, a fellow at the George W. Bush Institute, and a senior fellow at the Goldwater Institute. His work has been published in scholarly journals, such as the *Economics of Education Review*, *Education Finance and Policy*, and the *British Journal of Political Science*, in policy journals, such as *Education Next*, *Teachers College Record*, and the *Peabody Journal of Education*, and in popular outlets, such as the *Wall Street Journal*, the *Washington Post*, and *USA Today*. He is the coauthor of *Education Myths: What Special-Interest Groups Want You to Believe about Our Schools—and Why It Isn't So* (Rowman & Littlefield, 2005).

Matthew Ladner is director of research and policy at the Foundation for Excellence in Education, a senior fellow at the Goldwater Institute. He is also a former vice president of research at Goldwater. Before joining Goldwater, Ladner was director of state projects at the Alliance for School Choice, where he provided support and resources for state-based school choice efforts. Ladner has written numerous studies on school choice, charter schools, and special education reform.

Paul E. Peterson is the Henry Lee Shattuck Professor of Government and director of the Program on Education Policy and Governance at Harvard University, a senior fellow at the Hoover Institution, and editor-in-chief of *Education Next*. He is the coauthor of *The Education Gap: Vouchers and Urban Schools* (Brookings Institution, 2002).

Sheldon Richman is editor of *The Freeman*, published by the Foundation for Economic Education. He is the author of *Separating School and State: How to Liberate America's Families* (Future of Freedom Foundation, 1994) as well as papers and articles critical of government-run schools published by the Cato Institute and other organizations. When his children were of school age he was active in the homeschool community of central Arkansas.

C. Bradley Thompson is the BB&T Research Professor at Clemson University and executive director of the Clemson Institute for the Study of Capitalism. He is the author of *John Adams and the Spirit of Liberty* (University Press of Kansas, 1998).

James Tooley is professor of education policy and director of the E.G. West Centre at Newcastle University. He is the author of *The Beautiful Tree: A Personal Journey into How the World's Poorest People are Educating Themselves* (Cato Institute, 2009).

Index